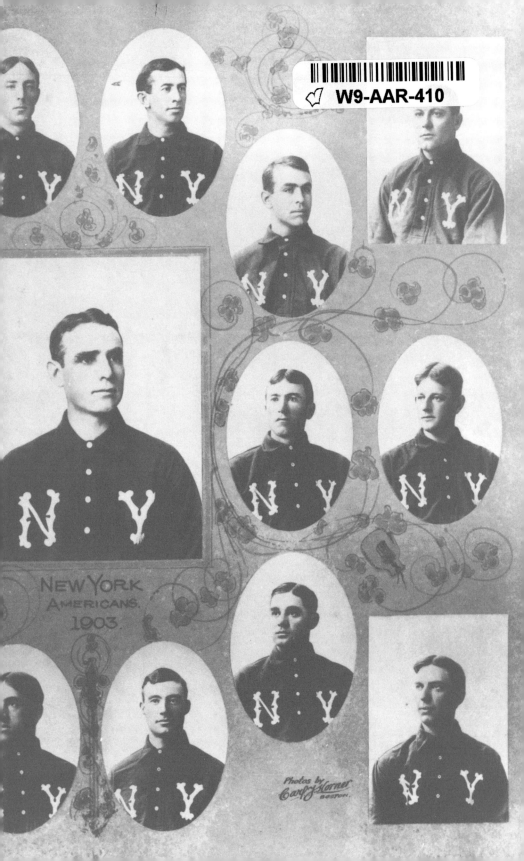

NEW YORK
AMERICANS.
1903.

Photos by
Canr J. Horner
BOSTON.

THE YEAR
THEY CALLED OFF
THE
WORLD SERIES
A TRUE STORY

THE YEAR THEY CALLED OFF THE WORLD SERIES

A TRUE STORY

BENTON STARK

AVERY PUBLISHING GROUP INC.

Garden City Park, New York

Cover Designers: Rudy Shur and Janine Eisner-Wall
In-House Editor: Cynthia J. Eriksen
Typesetter: Coghill Book Typesetting Co., Richmond, Virginia

Library of Congress Cataloging-in-Publication Data

Stark, Benton.
    The year they called off the World Series : a true story / Benton
Stark.
      p. cm.
    Includes bibliographical references and index.
    ISBN 0-89529-480-X : $17.95
    1. World series (Baseball)—History. 2. New York (N.Y.)—History.
I. Title.
GV878.4.S73 1991
796.357′646—dc20   91-6496
                                                              CIP

Printed in the United States of America

10 9 8 7 6 5 4 3 2 1

Contents

To my wife, Melinda, who sat through so many games trying hard to see the ghosts of baseball past. Thanks for the love, understanding, courage, and good humor.

Acknowledgements

Among the foot soldiers in the army of really helpful people who are never sufficiently acknowledged are those people who man the desks in public and private libraries and archives. They are expected to perform miracles on a daily basis for everyone with a dream in his head and a call slip in his hand. So, a sincere thanks to these terrific pathfinders, especially those who guided me through the collections of the New York Public Library and its journal and periodical annex; the Boston Public Library; the libraries of Columbia University, Hofstra University, Adelphi University, and C.W. Post College of Long Island University; and, especially, the library at the Baseball Hall of Fame.

In addition to those who helped me to gather information, I wish to express my gratitude to Cynthia Eriksen for her careful editing of the manuscript and to Rudy Shur for his enthusiasm, his encouraging words, and his belief in my ability to tell well a story worth telling.

On a very personal basis, I would like to thank some very special people who contributed to this enterprise and much else in my life. Thanks, first of all, to my mother, Stella, who always insisted that the most practical thing a person can do is tend to the space between his ears; to my son Ian, who helped me greatly with critical research in the Hall of Fame archives; to my son Roland, who inspired me with that primal baseball sound of a streaking fastball smacking into the hard leather of a catcher's mitt; and to Howard Ludecker, my Integrated Studies Program partner and good friend at North Shore High School, who kept me focused with his uncanny sense of the essential.

I also want to acknowledge those with whom I shared many exciting and unforgettable moments through the last decade coaching on playing fields from Levittown, New York, to Woonsocket, Rhode Island. Thanks Nick Vanore, Mike Sferrazza, Joe Morrissey, Marty Roddini, Pete Kerr, Pat Carr, Frank Valenti, John Rotondo, and Doug Yerkes.

Foreword

One of the greatest charms about our National Pastime is the ease with which we can read of games from nearly a century ago and still relate clearly to the events as though we were there. There were pinch runners for slowpokes, defensive replacements in oafish fielders, lordly umpires taking no gruff, and fans lining up early to get the best seats for the biggest games.

And oh, what characters we had then. The turn of the century brought forth not just a two-league rivalry, with the birth of the American League, but also a coming of age for Major League Baseball, when the question of respectability in the ballpark converged in opposition to accepted mores of the 1800s. There was Ban Johnson, founder of the American League, looking for clean play and backing up his umpires to the fullest. There was rough-and-tumble John McGraw, still a relatively young man of 30, bringing to this new era the down-and-dirty play of the nineteenth century, when men were men and college kids had no place in pro ball.

That McGraw even thought he could coexist running the

Baltimore Orioles for Johnson in the new league is properly viewed today, as it quickly was then, as absurd. That he returned to the National League to begin his long reign with the New York Giants is now historically engrossing. For he attempted to retain his olden values in the senior circuit, and did so with no less a flourish than refusing to lower himself to play a World Series in 1904. This, despite the fact there had been one in 1903, and many in different forms in the 1890s, in which he himself had participated.

But to sink into a 1904 showdown would be to honor Ban Johnson's league, to recognize that there was a bona fide rival for New York's sporting fans' attention, and to embrace the genteel style of play Johnson sought to introduce.

Of course, a victory could have given him bragging rights, and vindication of his style of play and decision to defect. But the brash McGraw cowered to the challenge, and, in some ways, caused a late conclusion to 1890s "Base Ball."

Ironically, much of what McGraw opposed was represented by his pitching ace, meal ticket, and roommate, Christy Mathewson, a refined college product who did much to bring civilized fans—even women—to ballparks. If the press, through its tirades over McGraw's stubbornness to play a 1904 Series, was failing to snap him into modern times, surely the presence of the chess-playing Matty would. It just took some time.

McGraw and Giants' owner John Brush were skilled business men. How dazzling it is to read of their decision to have visiting teams dress in their hotel, then travel to the Polo Grounds in horse-drawn carriages up Broadway; living advertisements for baseball (and convenient targets for the tomato throwers who lined the streets).

The events in this book, covering the early years of a two-league rivalry in New York, are resplendent with the games' most intriguing figures of the 1900s, perched in this awkward moment of history when two rivals faced off in public view, each looking to save face and make a larger statement.

McGraw and Brush did not win this one. They never did play a 1904 World Series. But the events, and the reaction they caused, saw to it that such a situation would never arise again. America was ready for two leagues, ready for a Fall Classic, and ready to embrace baseball as never before.

Baseball has enjoyed a surge of literature over the last quarter century, capturing so many of the great moments that have brought us to where we are today. My friend Ben Stark has greatly added to the game's literature with this tale of an event that *never* happened. We have no mementos of the 1904 World Series in Cooperstown, but the addition of this book to our Baseball Library will indeed fill a historian's void.

Edward W. Stack, President
National Baseball Hall of Fame and Museum
Cooperstown, New York

Preface

Every year, at World Series time, I've taken out my baseball record book to refamiliarize myself with World Series history. And, every year I've stumbled over the same line, 1904. Boston of the American League won the World Series in 1903. New York of the National League won the World Series in 1905. But, in 1904, no team won the World Series because none was held. Since I have long been aware that there has been a World Series in one form or another since the mid-1880s, I concluded that this could not have been the result of a casual decision. There had to be a good story here.

A few summers ago, having become temporarily disenchanted with the present game because of what ownership was doing to the New York Yankees—the only New York team that didn't run out of my town in the 1950s—I decided to crank up the microfilm in the Columbia University library to satisfy my curiosity about the 1904 season, the year there was no World Series. What I found was that there certainly could and should have been one. However, for reasons hav-

ing to do solely with the relationships among certain promi-
nent individuals, reasons that had no foundation in the pre-
vailing conditions of the game or nation, it was called off. At
this point, I was moved to take some notes, put my initial
findings together, and look further to reveal what I found to
be a fascinating page in baseball history.

In addition to the calling off of the World Series, what I
found in my research was a large number of extremely colorful personalities. Today, ballplayers are immediately con-
demned if they exhibit any kind of eccentricity. They are
expected to be members in good standing of the branches of
the corporate baseball business whose large checks they
cash. Back in 1904, there was little of this. Although ballplayers were the heroes of a substantial segment of the
American population, they were also suspected—often very
unfairly—of being somewhat unfit for normal society. If they
acted strangely, this was because of who they were in an
essential way. Even if officials wanted to spruce up the image
of the sport—and some did—there was a strong feeling that
no matter what rules and regulations were introduced,
nothing much could really be done with these presumably
scurrilous types. Consequently, ballplayers were afforded a
much greater range of behavior on and off the field. Obvious
indications of this latitude are the candidly descriptive nicknames earned by or at least pinned on many relatively unfet-
tered characters: for example, Norman "the Tabasco Kid"
Elberfeld, "Dirty Jack" Doyle, "Bad Bill" Dahlen, "Turkey
Mike" Donlin, John "Muggsy" or "Little Napoleon" McGraw,
Jesse "the Crab" Burkett, "Boileryard Bill" Clarke, "Wahoo
Sam" Crawford, "Ee-Yah Hughie" Jennings, "Noisy Johnny"
Kling, umpire Frank "Silk" O'Loughlin, and umpire "Blind
Bill" Emslie—to name just a few.

For me, frankly, it was nice to leave the cavernous concrete stadia of contemporary America with their ultragreen
carpets, red composition base cutouts, and computerized

electronic scoreboards, and reenter the old wooden–bleacher board grounds with their tufted sun-dried grass, mottled brown dirt infields, and simple paper scorecards.

It seems to me that things natural and a little imperfect provide a human environment of profound and authentic comfort. The game in 1904 was natural and a little imperfect, and I felt extremely at home in reading and writing about it. The age of human scale is, unhappily, fast slipping by. It was pleasant for me to go back to a time when it was still operating in full force and to dwell there in heart and mind for at least a little while.

THE YEAR THEY CALLED OFF THE WORLD SERIES

Prologue

To view baseball's World Series as just a sporting event is to confess a serious ignorance about this country's culture and sentiment. A vast number of people here look forward to the World Series as they do little else. It is the long-awaited, intensely dramatic showdown between two squads of outsized but intimately known experts of a proudly American athletic art form.

Virtually all American men have attempted to play the "national pastime" at some early, hopeful point in their lives, some with a degree of success, more with frustrating failure. Regardless of the extent of mastery, the feeling for baseball's place in our collective personality remains. It is one of those special elements that began to separate us from other nations relatively early in our history, and we enjoy owning its unique character, attempting to solve its arcane problems, and speaking its colorful language. We are envious of those among us who excel at it; and, for that reason, the "stars" who triumph on the highest of its levels are shifted upward in the great chain of being. When Japanese soldiers during the Second World War could think of nothing more injurious to say to American GIs than "Screw Babe Ruth," they were onto something. Violate what Babe Ruth represents as a symbol of American accomplishment and honor and a vital icon has been smashed. But to understand what was essential in the elevation of Ruth to icon status is to get back to what the World Series means. He was not just a great ball-player; nor was he just a synonym for the electrifying home run. He was the man whose virtues led the New York Yankees to all those World Series victories—and that's what ultimately counts!

The World Series, notes historian John Durant,

> lures United States presidents to the ball park, it crowds international events off the front pages of newspaper, it makes brothers of utter strangers standing three-deep at bars and it comes close to causing a nation-wide works stoppage in business and financial houses every October. It is reported by some 400 broadcasters and writers who annually turn out millions of words which describe in detail every move and gesture made on the ball field, as well as every sob and guffaw resounding in the clubhouse after the final game.

It even humbles its strongest participants, as New York Yankee catcher Bill Dickey, who experienced eight of them, admitted:

> The strain sets in just before the first game, and it lasts all the way through. My stomach gets upset. My lips break out in fever blisters. I lie awake nights thinking about what's going to happen. Maybe I don't look nervous during a Series, but I sure do feel it.
>
> The pressure stays on until the final putout. You don't want the agony prolonged for even one more day. That's the way you feel in the World Series. The

All-Star Game is nothing like it. You want to win it,
and you want to do good . . . but it isn't the World
Series. There's nothing like the World Series.

For a great many "fans" (from the word "fanatics") of a
team that has made it to the World Series, it eclipses pain-
fully drab routines and personal ineffectiveness. It entitles
those who have suffered with their heroes through the emo-
tionally undulating campaign to revel in the delicious
thought that they ultimately showed them all. They triumphed over all those presumptuous types from all those
other places who foolishly thought they were the best. For
them and for countless other loyal enthusiasts of the game
who temporarily switch allegiance in order to get in on the
fun of "rooting" and identifying with champions, to have
something interfere with the World Series would be unthinkable. Americans would not even permit world wars, a
prolonged economic depression, or even—most recently—a
fearsome and devastating earthquake to stop the playing of
the World Series.

However, this insistent attachment to baseball came at a
certain point in time, when the people came to feel that they
had a large measure of control over the game. There was,
however, another time.

At the very beginning of the twentieth century, America
was governed by personality and position much more than
by rules and regulations. Although there was the Constitution and all those statutes passed by Congress and lesser
institutions of all kinds, a determined man occupying a high
position could step over nearly any legal prohibition with
impunity. After all, Theodore Roosevelt, speaking from his
"bully pulpit," the White House, frankly recommended carrying a "big stick" as the most effective way to achieve an
objective—and this without any of the surprise or criticism
such a menacing statement would be greeted with today.
Public men were convinced they had to be publicly big to be

taken seriously. They had to have stout bodies to give the impression that they were established and prosperous because, it was believed, great accomplishments, great incomes, and great appetites all went together naturally. They had to have enormous town houses—even Fifth Avenue chateaux—and retreats in fancy summer colonies to display their booty conspicuously. They had to make extensive demands on those around them to exhibit supreme authority because the "boss," in those days, was virtually defined as the one who had the power, and therefore the right, to do the exploiting and to reap its benefits. And they had to have fast friendships and entrenched hatreds because the masculine image of the day featured a stubborn righteousness regarding personal feelings that did not allow for timid compromises.

This code of behavior was as true in the baseball business as it was in any other—perhaps truer, because the abrupt shifts up and down the league standings during the course of a long, tense season bred volatile personalities that felt compelled to battle furiously inning by inning, pitch by pitch, for the tiniest advantage. Dropping behind could mean being mired in a place where the championship, the only satisfying justification for all of the planning, hard work, and expense, became an impossible dream—and then the daily grind rapidly turned into a nightmare of futility. At the top of this ever-anxious baseball world were the club owners. When these magnates of the professional game peered into their mirrors, they saw themselves as Theodore Roosevelt, John D. Rockefeller, or J. P. Morgan—great public men who were not squeamish about wielding a "big stick" in order to conquer. The code of the day dictated that something of tremendous value to others in the baseball community might have to be smashed if it stood in the way of a magnate's personal goals and feelings. Actions such as these by people in power were not only accepted but deemed appropriate. The cardinal rule was to attend to one's private interests with a fierce determination and not to hesitate before the rules—especially ethical rules—because truly respected, successful men were single-minded and ruthless.

Under these circumstances, in 1904, in the heart of the age of relentless, selfish assertiveness, what, today, would be unthinkable was not only thought of but actually carried out. In that year, a couple of self-centered, driven men who owned and directed one well-positioned team decided, for purely personal reasons, to call off the World Series. Although there was some serious protest—after all, many fans and players, the two major leagues, and the reputation of the game itself stood to lose a great deal by this maddening act of proprietary arrogance—these men were able to get away with their decision because they were within their rights as understood in their era.

The principal characters, their personal quarrels and business interests, and the teams most directly involved in the calling off of the World Series were all located in New York. That one of baseball's most bizarre historic episodes should occur in this city should come as no surprise. Aside from the normally dynamic, if not agitated, qualities New York infuses into most of its residents and activities, this was the place where baseball, in its modern form, was born, nurtured, and grew up, and this was the place where the great majority of baseball's organizational schemes were drawn and redrawn right through the early twentieth century. Baseball and New York were married at an early age, and even Walter O'Malley of the "Los Angeles" Dodgers and Horace Stoneham of the "San Francisco" Giants, exhibiting some of the personal qualities of an earlier day, couldn't tear them apart—try as they might.

Here, then, is the story of a unique year in modern baseball history, 1904, the year they called off the World Series.

1.

Baseball and New York

Twenty-five-year-old Alexander Joy Cartwright, a sturdy 6-foot-2 socially correct Manhattanite who earned his living as a bank teller, was on a personal mission one day in the spring of 1845. Walking along the tree-lined Eastern Post Road, which ran through the villages of Yorkville and Harlem on the way to Boston, he turned and crossed a familiar meadow beneath the rocky Inclenberg projection of eastern mid-Manhattan's Murray Hill and made his way to Sunfish Pond, a polluted lake that had once enabled stagecoaches to water their horses before moving north of the city. Sunfish Pond would soon be drained and covered, establishing a more useful terrain for an area dominated by the steamcars of the New York and Harlem Railroad that bounded the meadow on the west and ran through a trench that turned out, ironically, to be Park Avenue. Cartwright was on his way to the field near Sunfish Pond where he and his colleagues played town ball, an American version of the old English game called rounders. This day, however, he brought along a diagram with some changes he had devised in the town ball-playing regulations. Referring to this diagram, he moved his companions to playing positions around a new ninety-foot square, or "diamond," and stationed the batter at the fourth base, "home," instead of in a separate box a few feet closer to first base, as the old rules had it. The bases were to be flat, not the traditional posts. There would be only three outfielders, and between second and third base there would be a new infielder, whom Cartwright called the shortstop. Only one catcher would be stationed behind the hitter, not two. From now on, outs would be recorded by tagging a base or a runner with the ball, not hitting or "soaking" him with it. Three outs would end a team's time at bat, rather than the enormously time-consuming requirement that the whole team get up every inning. A run apparently scored while a third out was made on a play where a batter or runner was forced to move toward first or any other of the bases no longer counted. And clear foul lines enclosed the playing field. The result of Cartwright's adjustments was the game we know as baseball. He, not Abner Doubleday, was "the man who invented baseball," as Harold Peterson calls him in his graphic account of that significant afternoon in 1845.

The Doubleday story would originate just after the turn of the century as the result of an imperious and impatient effort by Albert Spalding, the most powerful of baseball personages in the early twentieth century, to attach his beloved game to an American with all the right homespun origins and patriotic credentials to dispel the idea that baseball had its origins on English soil as "rounders," as some were accurately asserting. Insistent nationalists of the day, and Spalding was stridently one of them, tried to dissociate everything good in America from the Old World. While Cartwright, with some red, white, and blue elaboration here and there, might have done almost as nicely as Doubleday as the leading figure for his case, Spalding had little or no knowledge of the former's singular contribution and, so, arranged for a committee of baseball and political dignitaries—who also happened to be personal friends on whom he could rely—to assert what he hoped would be the final and distinctly American word in the debate on the origins of baseball. Based on the unexamined testimony of one elderly man's extremely questionable recollections of his school days in Cooperstown, Spalding declared that it was Abner Doubleday, later a Civil War hero taking part in the Union's defense of Fort Sumter, the Second Battle of Bull Run, Antietam, Fredericksburg, Chancellorsville, and Gettysburg, who authored the game in the gloriously native earth of a field in central New York State. Distinguished baseball historian Harold Seymour points out that for Doubleday to have done this when the Spalding Commission's 1907 report declared he did, the future major general would have had to have been AWOL from West Point, which he was attending at the time. "If he had any particular connection with the game," writes Seymour,

> it is not revealed in local histories or even in his own writings. Recalling his boyhood, Doubleday omits any mention of interest in baseball. Besides, Abraham G. Mills, chairman of the commission, had known Doubleday for years, dating from their association as soldiers in the Civil War; yet he never mentioned anything about Doubleday's alleged contribution to baseball prior to the publication of the [Abner] Graves [the elderly Cooperstown "witness"] statement.

Nevertheless, in time, organized baseball, with no further scrutiny or research of its own, gave the Spalding account its solid red brick endorsement by the location of its inspirational Hall of Fame, and the myth remains one of those points of "information" that the average American accepts as fact.

In September 1845, Cartwright suggested that the group of young men who frequented the Murray Hill baseball field organize a formal association. They agreed and formed the Knickerbocker Base Ball Club, named after the recently disbanded volunteer Knickerbocker Engine Company to which Cartwright and some of the others had belonged.

By this time, the Murray Hill playing area was threatened by Manhattan's rapid urbanization. Blocks of homes had appeared on Third Avenue, signaling the need to find a new open space for the Knickerbockers' baseball pastime. Cartwright persuaded his friends to examine the "Elysian Fields," in rural Hoboken, New Jersey, as a possible new site. One afternoon in October, the Knickerbockers took the Barclay Ferry across the Hudson River and viewed the expanse of greenery owned by Colonel John Stevens, an engineer who busied himself by designing steamboats and steam railroads. He promoted the use of the Elysian Fields as a way of stimulating the use of his ferry service. It was here that the Knickerbockers first wore the flannel uniforms and caps that would establish the style for baseball teams thereafter.

Back in Manhattan, other baseball clubs, inspired by the Knickerbockers, were beginning to form and play among themselves and against each other. In the early summer of 1851, the Washington Club began playing on the St. George cricket grounds up the Eastern Post Road in Harlem. They eagerly invited the Knickerbockers to play two games on their home field. Predictably, however, the newer squad lost both to the more experienced players. The Washington Club renamed itself the Gotham Club and, in a short while, became a force in the rapidly expanding world of baseball in the New York metropolitan area. In 1854, the Eagle and Empire clubs began playing, as did the Excelsiors—or the "Jolly Young Bachelors Club"—in the independent city of

Brooklyn. The next year the Putnam Club was organized in Williamsburgh, and the Star Club in Hoboken. All of these baseball playing associations consisted of young middle-class gentlemen who enjoyed the hearty social as well as athletic aspects of playing against each other. For example, any game at the Elysian Fields would be followed by a friendly visit to McCarty's Tavern, and any game at St. George's grounds would be followed by the same sort of cheer in the Red House Tavern.

Nevertheless, as much as they would have liked to, the middle class could not keep the joys of baseball and its associated benefits a secret. The working class quickly discovered the excitement of the game and began to organize its own clubs. In 1856, two plebeian baseball organizations were formed, the Eckfords of Greenpoint and the Atlantics of Jamaica. "Suddenly baseball became no less than a mania," writes Harold Peterson, historian of these early days.

> Every young man in the city must play and must belong to a club. Throngs of them rose at four and five in the morning to practice before work. They talked and thought of almost nothing else. Employers who had previously eschewed employees who drank or gambled now began asking prospective clerks whether they played ball. (But sometimes the boss too caught the disease and actively sought ball players.) Such wage-workers eventually formed scores and hundreds of baseball clubs.

In 1858, representatives of twenty-two of these baseball clubs, including the Knickerbockers, Gothams, Eagles, and Empires, met at the Bowery headquarters of the Gothams and created the first baseball league, the National Association of Base Ball Players. This association of amateurs, young men who played the game solely because they loved it, would remain the governing body for the next thirteen years.

In that initial year, the first championship series—a primitive World Series—was held between all–star teams from New York and Brooklyn. The site chosen was neutral Long Island. New York area fans responded ardently. Nearly 1,500 clogged the roads and the Flushing Railroad to reach the Fashion Race Course in West Flushing (Corona). The fifty cents they paid to enter the grounds was probably the first fee charged for a baseball game. New York won this championship series two games to one; however, Brooklyn dominated what became an annual confrontation through the next decade. It was not until the Unions of Morrisania—from the Bronx—triumphed in 1867 that Brooklyn's hold on the championship was loosened. Until then, either the Brooklyn Atlantics or the Brooklyn Eckfords won what was called the "whip pennant." The real significance of the Fashion Race Course series, asserts Harold Seymour, "was the interest it stirred and the thousands of new converts it made for the game. Although New York remained the capital city of baseball, its popularity was spreading like a brush fire to other parts of the country."

In 1860, just before the Civil War, the Excelsiors of Brooklyn helped to intensify this brush fire by touring through New York State and cities in surrounding states. By the time of the Civil War, baseball was understood and played by a large number of people throughout the country. Still, at this stage, its strength remained within a relatively short radial distance of its home base, New York City and environs. Even diehard town ball players in New England were abandoning their old "Massachusetts game" in favor of baseball—which they and others sometimes called the "New York game."

During the Civil War, baseball was played by a great many northern troops and even by some southern ones in camps and prisons. Nicholas E. Young, later the fourth president of the National League, remembered the New York 27th

Regiment turning its attention to baseball whenever it could. This was Young's introduction to the game. Captain James Hall of the Alabama 24th Regiment related that he and his men played baseball while waiting for enemy General William T. Sherman to commit his forces to their notorious course of deadly action through Georgia. Interregimental games were held and one of these between Duryea's New York Zouaves and a team selected from other units was witnessed on Christmas Day, 1862, by 40,000 soldiers. Back on the Elysian Fields, on October 21, 1861, 10,000 spectators attended the so-called "Silver Ball Match" between all-stars from New York and Brooklyn. The Eckfords of Brooklyn were so little inconvenienced by the war that they completed their entire schedule and were acknowledged as the baseball champions of 1863. When peace came, a tremendous proliferation of organized clubs occurred, so that the attendance records at the annual conventions of the National Association of Base Ball Players rose dramatically from 30 in 1964, to 91 in 1865, to 202 in 1866. There was no doubt about it—baseball had become what people were already calling it: "the national pastime."

Whatever the intent of the original gentlemen's clubs or the demands of the National Association, baseball's great popularity invited ideas about how to make it profitable, thereby inevitably altering the game. It might be a pastime for some, but for others it became a living. In 1862, William Cammeyer, the owner of the Union Club's playing field in the Williamsburgh section of Brooklyn, enclosed it and charged ten cents admission. The following year, the Unions demanded a portion of the receipts, and Cammeyer, having discovered an easy income, agreed to share the wealth. Furthermore, although it was strictly against the National Association's code, players began to make money the reason for performing for a certain team. The first unofficial professional player seems to have been the young pitching ace of the Brooklyn Excelsiors, Jim Creighton. But the twenty-one-year-old Creighton died mysteriously, in 1862, as he hurriedly rounded the bases after hitting what would have been a home run. His club buried him in style in Brooklyn's Greenwood Cemetery, with a large tombstone bearing crossed bats, a scorebook, a base, a baseball cap, and a scroll with the word "Excelsior" on it, all under a granite baseball symbolically positioned at the summit.

Baseball's route toward a financial preoccupation could be seen in the path taken by the New York Mutuals. The team began in the days of the old gentlemen's clubs, drawing on the volunteer firemen of the Mutual Hook and Ladder Company No. 1. During the 1860s it fell under the command of William Marcy Tweed, the infamous "Boss" of Tammany Hall, New York City's scandalous Democratic Party political machine. Tweed bought Cincinnati's second baseman, Charley Sweasy, with a large salary and then put the rest of the team on the city payroll as "employees" of the street cleaning department. In 1868, the officially amateur Mutuals had a $15,000 treasury to draw upon. Although the Mutuals still titularly represented New York while in the National Association, in fact, they played their home games in Brooklyn on Cammeyer's Union Grounds.

By 1871, the jumping or "revolving" of professional players from one team to another for a greater salary had reached the point of being enormously disruptive. On March 17 of that year, at New York's Colliers Rooms on Broadway, a conference of representatives of the leading baseball clubs created a new National Association. This one would be called, straightforwardly, the National Association of Professional Base Ball Players. For the first time, baseball was recognized as a business. Alexander Joy Cartwright and the values of his time had now been forgotten in all ways.

The new National Association quickly gained a reputation for allowing too much gambling, with the associated charges of "hippodroming" or throwing games for money.

Furthermore, in the way of serious problems, Boston thoroughly dominated the league and caused sharp resentment in many cities. Most resentful of all was William A. Hulbert, president of the Chicago White Stockings. Since Boston had attracted a number of midwestern boys eastward, Hulbert decided to reverse the flow, and, while the 1875 season was still in progress, secretly signed four of Boston's stars to Chicago contracts for the next season. The secret quickly hit the newspapers, which had already established that mutually advantageous relationship with baseball in which both got the public's attention and money by means of vendible gossip. It seemed likely that since the Chicago organization had violated the most fundamental of all rules—tampering with another club's players, and its best players at that—the Boston management would ask the National Association for the extreme but suitable penalty of expulsion.

Hulbert, however, had a plan, which he laid out with the help of one of the former Boston stars whom he lured to Chicago, pitcher Albert Goodwill Spalding. Cutting short his honeymoon, Spalding stayed at Hulbert's house, where the two of them dreamed up the National League of Professional Baseball Clubs—not players, but "clubs." This league was going to be run not by those who understood what to do on the field but by those who understood what to do in the office—the business office. Endeavoring to make everyone forget that the original motivation for designing a new circuit was to rescue their club from the oblivion into which the old one was about to toss it, Hulbert and Spalding would insist that the weaknesses of the National Association made it necessary to establish the National League, and to establish it on a different, more businesslike basis. Harold Seymour likened their public relations position to those

> friends of the new American Constitution of 1789 [who] constantly praised the work of the Founding Fathers and blackened the previous period when

America was governed under the Articles of Confederation; so the men of the National League, particularly when under attack by rival organizations or their own dissatisfied players, conveniently forgot their less worthy motives. . . . The constant refrain was, "The National League was organized as a necessity, to rescue the game from its slough of corruption and disgrace."

Among the delegates from the eastern clubs meeting in the Grand Central Hotel in New York City on February 2, 1876, to put the finishing touches on the National League were representatives of the New York Mutuals. During that first year of National League play, the strong central direction of the enterprise destroyed the New York Mutuals. Attempting to save money by not making a late western trip, the club violated a primary rule concerning the integrity of the schedule and was punished by exclusion from the League. The New York area, birth and rearing place of baseball, had to wait until 1880 for a high-level team, the New York Metropolitans, to be organized. Although not a member of the National League, the Mets played 151 games in 1881, the most ever taken on, to that point, in the game's history.

After six years as the only major circuit of baseball clubs, the National League received word that a competitor had been organized in Cincinnati. In that city, on November 1, 1881, delegates from six cities, including Brooklyn, met to create the American Association of Baseball Clubs. The major business interest represented was beer manufacturing—four of the clubs would be owned by brewers. The organizers of what was intended to be a new major league wanted a New York entry and attempted to work something out with the New York Mets. However, the Mets' management decided to wait a year and see how successful this venture was before making a commitment. Meanwhile, the American Association signed ballplayers unhappy with their National League clubs and enticed fans with promises of a twenty-five-cent admission rather than the League's fifty cents, beer at the ballpark, and Sunday baseball wherever not prevented by local blue laws. Because of their six-day work week, urban laborers found it nearly impossible to attend baseball games during the week or on Saturdays, and many of them really enjoyed their beer when they could find the leisure to get to it. So a "wet" Sunday at the ballpark was a dream come true for them—and for the keepers of the American Association coffers. In fact, the six clubs of the Association made good money in 1882, its first season, and decided to expand to eight clubs in 1883.

The establishment of this rival league was not contested by Abraham G. Mills, the new president of the National League. In fact, he quickly arranged a peace meeting with representatives of the Association and of the Northwestern League, a large "minor league"—that is, one that operated on a more modest financial level, recognized an inferior status in terms of its caliber of play, and concentrated on developing players for sale to the "major leagues." The biggest problem of the minor leagues was convincing the major leagues to honor their player contracts and stay out of their profitable baseball areas. The three-way negotiations were held at the Victoria Hotel, on Broadway at Twenty-seventh Street, New York City. What resulted was the so-called National Agreement, which established basic principles of cooperation that have governed organized baseball for most of the rest of its history. It protected every club's contracts and established that each club would have firm control over its players by what was known as the "reserve rule." This was a device first established in 1879 by the National League that allowed a club to bind five of its players, at first, and then virtually all of its players to perform for itself and no one else. Initially, it was a matter of a collective conspiracy among the league's clubs, but eventually it became a legal trap in the form of a contract clause that projected a player's ownership from the present year's signed agreement into successive years. Despite its questionable morality, it was, nevertheless, an effective way to keep players from "revolving." Furthermore, minimum salaries were agreed upon for both major and minor league levels, and the three organizations promised to uphold each other's suspensions and expulsions, and to respect each other's territories.

Although the New York Mets were not directly involved in all these arrangements, they were still doing very well. In 1881, playing their home games at the Westchester Polo Club—often against National League teams—they were winners on the field and on the books, taking in $30,000 in gate receipts. The following year, the owner and manager of the Mets, John B. Day and Jim Mutrie, respectively, joined with another club expelled from the National League for not finishing its schedule, the Philadelphia Athletics, in a two-team league which they called the League Alliance. Together they lobbied the National League to consider their reinstatement. When the National League held its seventh annual convention in Providence, Rhode Island, in December 1882, Day and Philadelphia's owner and former star infielder, Alfred J. Reach, formally applied for membership and were accepted. Deciding to take advantage of the fact that there were two major leagues and no rule forbidding owners from having a team in each league, Day and Mutrie put the Mets in the American Association and a new team called the Gothams, soon to be known as the Giants, in the National League. The future Giants would draw most of their initial roster from the National League club they replaced, the Troy Haymakers. In 1883 New York went from having no teams officially playing on the major league level to having two.

By 1885, it was clear that New York baseball fans preferred to watch the "Giants," so-called because of their size and the elevated amount of spirit with which they played the game. Therefore, Day shifted his better Met players to his National League club, angering the American Association owners. After the sale of the Mets to Erastus Wiman of the Staten Island Amusement Company and the Staten Island Transit System, and the subsequent scheduling of games in out-of-the-way Staten Island as a way of stimulating the local ferry business, the Association owners, following the 1887 season, forced the surrender of the club's franchise. These developments were truly curious in light of the great success the Mets had had in 1884, winning the American Association pennant and taking part in the very first completed World Series between the two great major circuits. (An effort had been made to play a World Series the previous year, but hard feelings between the leagues caused the American Association to pull out of it.) Although the New York Mets lost the 1884 World Series to the Providence Grays in three straight games, the team did exceedingly well to qualify for the championship series from which fourteen other teams had been eliminated.

In addition to the star Met players, manager Jim Mutrie was also transferred to the Giants. However, Mutrie found a superior field leader on the Giant squad and restricted himself to the business end of National League baseball in New York. The man who took over the actual direction of the players was John Montgomery Ward. "Monte" Ward had been one of the first celebrated curve ball pitchers and has been credited with the design of the raised pitching mound. He had been the ace of the Providence Grays for several years, posting the phenominal record of 49–17 in 1878, pitching a perfect game in 1880 and an eighteen-inning shutout in 1882. But, by 1883, he had developed arm trouble. Nevertheless, refusing to see the end of his illustrious career, he converted himself into a fine shortstop, learned to switch-hit, and developed strategies that made him the most feared base runner in the league.

Not only was Ward capable of acquiring new skills on the ball field, but he gave ample evidence of his learning capacity in the classroom as well. Taking advantage of being in New York, Ward attended Columbia College and Columbia Law School and earned degrees at both. With his appreciation for what was legally as well as morally right, Ward, in October 1885, assumed the leading role in creating the Brotherhood of Professional Baseball Players, an organization that hoped to alter the harsh treatment of major league players as mere objects of club profit. Players at this time received no payment for time lost to injury or illness and were effectively blacklisted if they caused any trouble.

In addition to the shift of control from the players on the field to the owners in their well-appointed offices, the game itself had changed substantially since the days of Alexander Joy Cartwright and the gentlemen New York Knicker-bockers. The Playing Rules Committee of the two major leagues would meet between seasons—separately from 1882 to 1886, and then jointly—to review the effectiveness of the playing code. In 1876, a rule change made a batted ball foul unless it passed third or first base in fair territory. Until then, any ball touching anywhere in fair territory first was fair. In 1879, a rule change made a batted ball not caught on a fly in foul territory nothing more than a foul. Until then, catching a batted ball on the first bounce in foul territory constituted a putout—even as a result of a foul tip. The pitching distance had been forty-five feet since the days of the Knickerbockers until the Rules Committee moved it back to fifty feet in 1881 and created a seven- by four-foot box in which the pitcher could roam. Then, in 1886, an added regulation compelled the pitcher to keep one foot on the rear line of this box, now reduced to five and a half by four feet, to prevent the confusing running deliveries that had come into vogue. Furthermore, pitchers, who had been limited to relatively slow underhand tosses, were allowed, despite great fears of the likely danger to hitters, to whip the ball sidearm in 1883 and overhand in 1884. After experimenting with all sorts of formulas for the count, it was decided, in 1889, that the fairest one for all concerned was four balls and three strikes. That same year, for the first time, the right of a batter to run past first base without jeopardy—as long as he didn't make any effort to go to second—was sanctioned. Before 1889, substitutions could be made only with the permission of the opposing manager, who could refuse to give it. At times a manager would withhold his permission even when a player had apparently broken a bone. In 1889 each team was allowed one substitution; by the following year, two. It was not until 1891 that substitution restrictions were removed altogether.

The attire of the players was changing too. Although the basic uniform remained the same, the socks took on greater importance, especially after the 1876 National League assignment of team colors. Many teams such as the Providence and Louisville Grays, the St. Louis Browns, the Chicago White Stockings, and the old Cincinnati and Boston Red Stockings owed their nicknames to the color of their hosiery. Canvas shoes with cleats were first worn by the Harvard College team in 1877, but old-fashioned leather proved to be a more durable material for hard-running and hard-sliding professional ballplayers.

Gloves came into use slowly because of the question about the manliness of resorting to such an overt pain-saving device. The first ones, in the mid-1870s, were fingerless and made of buckskin. Although there would be old-timers who would continue to refuse to wear a glove into the 1890s, influential playing legends such as Al Spalding, George Wright, and Al Reach, who were, not so coincidentally, also the leading figures in the sporting goods business, promoted its use, and it soon became standard equipment. Spalding, by now the most celebrated of the game's figures, was especially instrumental in removing the fear of ridicule involved in glove wearing. Rejecting the deceptive flesh-colored variety that some had fearfully slipped on, Spalding appeared at first base with a no-nonsense black glove, visible to all.

Changes in catchers' equipment were taking place as well. In the early days, catchers stood well behind the hitter. Despite having a cushion of a dozen feet or so, catchers were still in danger of being hit and took to wearing a wide rubber band stretched over the face or simply a rubber mouthpiece. But when catchers began to move closer to the hitter in the mid-1870s, there was a clear need for better protection. In 1873, Harvard's James Tyng, having been made a bit shy because of several foul tips in the face, got help from teammate Fred W. Thayer, who designed the first catcher's mask after an old fencing face cage. This was clearly such a good idea that professional catchers thankfully and readily adopted the mask, making it an accepted part of the baseball scene overnight. Chest protectors began to appear in the mid-1880s, but shin guards would await the twentieth century, when they were first hidden under stockings and pants because of the old fear of exhibiting a lack of manly courage.

Umpires had been paid as early as the 1850s; however, when the National League was organized in 1876, it established a five-dollar-a-game wage, paid by the home club, for the one umpire who controlled the whole field all nine innings. Most of the umpires were financially impoverished former ballplayers who, as baseball historian Robert Smith notes, "ate and drank with the players, [and] even played catch with them on the field. . . . They were insulted, berated, and punched in the nose; and they dared not protest too loudly lest the few dollars their umpiring brought be snatched away." When the American Association began playing in 1882, President Denny McKnight appointed a specially chosen staff of umpires, dressed them in blue coats and caps, and paid them season salaries through his office. The next year, the National League copied this rational scheme.

By the 1880s, baseball had developed its own language spoken by all of its fanatical afficionados. English-born Henry Chadwick, the game's first newspaper writer and statistician, and inventor of the box score, published a lexicon of special baseball terms. In it "Father" Chadwick, as he came to be known for his guardianship of the cause, defined such already standard words and phrases as assists, grounders, pop-ups, double plays, overthrows, and passed balls. And Thomas Lawson's book *The Krank: His Language and What It Means* served as a guide for the comprehension of the many who, by this time, had become so completely hooked by the game that they had a hard time communicating with the uninitiated. "Krank" was the term then commonly used for this phenomenon, the word coming from "krankheit," German for malady—in this case, of the head. Kranks, according to Lawton, could be incredible pests, torturing horsecar passengers with their boisterous chatter on the way to the game, and ticket sellers, gatekeepers, newspaper writers, players, and umpires while too energetically watching the game.

At the end of the 1880s, glory came to New York in the form of two National League pennants. In 1888, under the field leadership of catcher William "Buck" Ewing—"Monte" Ward resigned the captaincy because of a dispute over salary—the Giants, deliberately uniformed in menacing black, finished a full nine games ahead of the second-place White Stockings. They then faced the St. Louis Browns, winners of the American Association pennant, in the World Series, the fifth of these postseason interleague championship challenges that already constituted a traditional and eagerly awaited conclusion to the major league season. The New

Yorkers quickly won the needed five games in the best-of-nine series but agreed to play added exhibition contests, finishing the great fall spectacle with a 6–4 record.

Not only had this team captured the hearts of ordinary baseball fans in New York, but it became the darling of the big city's renowned show business set. Many of the celebrities who appeared on the stages of the "Great White Way" could be spotted at the benefit given the victorious baseball heroes in the State Theatre. Among those paying ten dollars a seat—with all proceeds going to the players as a substantial token of appreciation—was William De Wolfe Hopper, who had just begun his celebrated recitation of "Casey at the Bat," a light but poignant narrative poem written by Ernest L. Thayer for the *San Francisco Examiner* earlier in the year. It immediately became a great favorite among the Giant players. Hopper recalled that the first time "Buck" Ewing heard the tale, his "gallant mustachios" gave "a single nervous twitch," as he stifled the feeling of horror at the idea that "the mighty Casey," as reliable a player as the Giant captain himself, could have struck out in the clutch.

For the six years of their existence, the Giants played in the Polo Grounds' East Diamond just off Central Park, with Fifth Avenue behind home plate, West 110th Street beyond left field, West 112th Street beyond right field, and the West Diamond—where the Mets formerly played—on the other side of center field. After the Giants had won the World Series, the New York City government decided to close the Polo Grounds in order to complete a traffic circle on 110th Street. When the 1889 season began, Giant fans had to travel to Staten Island to see their team play. However, by July, the club returned to Manhattan, moving into a new Polo Grounds way up on the East Side between 155th and 157th streets just before the Harlem River. Here the center and right fielders would have to negotiate one of the steepest embankments in any ballpark ever. Another difficulty the

Giants faced in their new surroundings was an unusually heavy September rainfall, which flooded their unsettled grounds and caused the postponement of a number of home games while their rivals for the National League pennant, the Boston Beaneaters, continued to play and win. Nevertheless, on the last day of the season, the Giants defeated the Cleveland Spiders while the Beaneaters lost to the Pittsburg Pirates ("Pittsburg" was how the city officially spelled its name between 1884 and 1908 because the post office thought the "h" was superfluous), and, in what had been the circuit's tightest and most exciting pennant race to date, the New Yorkers claimed the National League flag for the second consecutive year.

The pennant winner in the American Association in 1889 was a team called the Brooklyn Dodgers, which played its home games in Red Hook's Washington Park, at Fourth Avenue and Third Street, site of the ill-fated American Revolutionary battle of Long Island. This was its sixth season in the league, and its triumph was also a narrow one, a slim two-game advantage over the defending champs, the St. Louis Browns. The name "Dodgers" came from the independent city of Brooklyn's ubiquitous trolley cars that compelled pedestrians to learn how to avoid, or dodge, them agilely or suffer serious grief. So, Brooklyn's Dodgers faced New York's Giants in the 1889 World Series, the first of the numerous and legendary baseball wars within the metropolitan area that would one day, when the nominal means of transportation had been installed beneath the streets and bay, be called the "subway series." For now, the horse and trolley car, elevated railway, or Brooklyn Bridge series might be an appropriate name. In what was to be a best-of-nine-games confrontation, the Dodgers broke on top winning three of the first four—two of them shortened by the umpire's controversial decision that it was too dark to continue play. Nevertheless, just as the season began badly for the Giants and then corrected itself so that they were able to emerge league champions, their initial tough luck in the World Series suddenly changed and they piled up five consecutive wins to take the World Series six games to three.

So thoroughly had baseball captured the interest and affections of Americans in a half-century that, from time to time, some of its more venturesome entrepreneurs tested the potential for a baseball market abroad. Back in 1874, two of these, the ever-active Albert Spalding and George Wright, decided to take two American baseball teams on a six-week tour of England to spread the game that they loved and profited from so handsomely. Wright returned greatly disappointed, but not Spalding. His "strong sense of moral mission," writes baseball historian David Quentin Voigt, "which assumed that the world must come to be like America, never flagged." In the spring of 1888, Spalding decided to resume the mission. He had taken the game across the Atlantic; now he would bring it to the people of the Pacific. Ten players from the Chicago White Stockings and ten players from other major league teams, to be called the "All-Americans," would travel to Hawaii, New Zealand, Australia, Ceylon, and Egypt, then shift westward to give the English a second chance to appreciate America's pastime. After a stop in Ireland, baseball's missionaries would return home for a final exhibition game or two on home soil and then begin their regular season's play. The travel went according to plan, but the appreciation did not. Somehow, baseball just didn't interest tropical villagers or urbanites whose ancient cultures were profoundly different from the one that was so curiously proclaiming itself in colorful shirts, knee pants, and spiked shoes. Not that Spalding hadn't tried very hard to evoke an affection for the game on foreign soil, because he certainly had. Upon the group's arrival in Cairo, he posted a notice in the Hotel d'Orient to inform his players and the local population of his plans:

The Chicago and All-American teams, composing the Spalding Baseball Party, will please report in the hotel office in uniform, promptly at ten o'clock tomorrow morning. We shall leave the hotel at that hour, camels having been provided for the All-Americans and donkeys for the Chicago players, with carriages for the balance of the party. The Pyramids will be inspected, the Sphinx visited, and a game played upon the desert nearby, beginning at two o'clock.

Two hundred local people showed up to sell coins and alleged historical treasures. The players took photos on the Sphinx and then proceeded to play a game, which was continually interrupted by exhausting efforts to convince the few curious Egyptian onlookers to surrender foul balls that shot off into the desert.

Among the players on the "All-American" team was "Monte" Ward, New York Giant shortstop and leader of the Brotherhood of Professional Baseball Players. As soon as the tour group returned through the Port of New York, Ward was informed that an important development had taken place while he was away. The National League had adopted the so-called "Classification Plan," devised by John Tomlinson Brush, owner of the Indianapolis Hoosiers, to place each player in one of five groups according to "habits, earnestness, and special qualifications" and pay him within a reduced and tightly constricted salary range. This was objectionable on two grounds: the serious limitations on a player's income and the power handed management to judge a player's personal behavior. It seemed obvious that the league was trying to take advantage of Ward's absence since the Brotherhood's very able president was too far away to respond, as he certainly would have done vehemently. While no action was taken by the Brotherhood during the 1889 season, Ward made use of these summer months to find the financial backers that would allow the players to leave the

National League and American Association en masse, in 1890, for an organization of their own, a players' league. The justification for this revolutionary undertaking was written by Ward and handed to the press in early November:

> There was a time when the league stood for integrity and fair dealing; today it stands for dollars and cents. Once it looked to the elevation of the game and an honest exhibition of the sport; today its eyes are upon the turnstile. Men have come into the business for no other motive than to exploit it for every dollar in sight. . . . Players have been bought and sold, and exchanged as though they were sheep instead of American citizens. "Reservation" became with them another name for property right in the player. By a combination among themselves, stronger than the strongest trust, they were able to enforce the most arbitrary measures. . . . Even the disbandment . . . of a club did not free the players from the octopus clutch, for they were then peddled around to the highest bidder.

Although the Classification Plan was dropped by the National League at its annual meeting that year, the organization of the Players' League went ahead as planned. Colonel Edwin A. McAlpin, a New York real estate tycoon, was elected president of the new major league, which moved right into cities already possessing National League and American Association franchises. Actually, this was the second time that organized baseball had been challenged. The first time was back in 1884, when the Union Association attempted to break into professional baseball at the top level. However, this operation, the child of Henry V. Lucas, scion of a wealthy St. Louis family, never drew enough talent to make for a balanced, major league-caliber pennant race. Lucas's St. Louis Maroons totally dominated the sorry competition and after a short while, few remembered much about the one-season Union Association. The Players'

League, however, began with an extremely rich pool of established ballplayers and, if the business end had held up, could have compelled the baseball public to recognize that it was by far the premier organization. Unfortunately, the strength of the Players' League was tested by the management capability of the National League, which established a "war committee" chaired by the clever and tough-minded Al Spalding. The "war committee," with the assistance of the press it had long courted and almost totally won over, did an effective job in convincing the public that baseball owed the National League a great debt for having developed and morally corrected the game. Incredibly enough, the National League succeeded in holding on to its image as the real major league, despite the location of baseball talent during the season. "Father" Chadwick, editor of the *Spalding Guide*, the National League's semi-official statistical organ, blasted the Brotherhood for its revolutionary language and unconscionable lack of gratitude toward the organization that had provided so many of its members with an opportunity to make a living playing the national game on the highest and cleanest of professional levels. The pro-National League baseball press "waved the bloody shirt," focusing on "Monte" Ward as the villainous mastermind of the "secessionist" venture—a conception still met with righteous anger by Union loyalists who saw the Civil War as the murderous calamity barely and imperfectly concluded. In the end, the Players' League, which should have been able to survive the counterattack mounted by the National League and eventually overcome it, collapsed. Its weakness was primarily in the men who financed it. They held meetings with the National League's "war committee" to protect themselves, and, in doing so, instilled a justifiable fear of double-dealing in the minds of the players. New York was the location of the numerous meetings between the rival leagues' money men. The rumors darting all over this city and beyond soon destroyed what little faith remained about the viability of an operation that was originally to combine capital and labor in a harmonious and profitable sports-business partnership and to treat those who provided the skill and entertainment on the field with the respect they had long been denied by their former exploitative employers.

Of all the National League clubs injured by the Players' League during the vicious campaign of 1890, the team hurt the most was the New York Giants. Most of the champion 1889 squad threw their lot in with "Monte" Ward and the Brotherhood, leaving the Giants struggling for respectability. Convinced that a weak New York franchise was unhealthy for its standing, the National League worked a deal whereby the better ballplayers on John T. Brush's shaky Indianapolis Hoosiers were sold to New York, with Brush promised proper compensation from the league after the season was over and the battle against the Players' League won. John B. Day also received a very substantial amount of monetary assistance from other National League owners after he informed them that he was in such financial trouble that he might be forced to sell out to the Brotherhood's New York organization. "It was pretty costly," remarked Al Spalding, "but that prompt act saved the National League, and, by saving it, the future of professional baseball in this country was, in my opinion, also saved."

By the end of the season, the financial backers of the Players' League were prepared to sell their interests to Spalding and the National League owners. Only slightly more alive than the waylaid Players' League was the American Association. It had tried its best to stay out of the crossfire but failed. Its players had also been taken by the Brotherhood's teams, and its clubs, at each other's throat over policy and the league presidency, began to defect to the stronger National League. Pittsburg had gone that way in 1887, Cleveland in 1889, and, in 1890, Cincinnati and

Brooklyn, its defending champion, jumped ship, too. American Association owners, just before the start of the 1891 season, decided to withdraw from the National Agreement. In retaliation, National League clubs were not permitted to play any exhibition games with the moribund Association, a move that deprived it of what little extra revenue it could have collected in its desperate effort to survive as a serious professional baseball league.

By the fall of 1891, it was all over for the National League's only rival. American Association clubs were bought out and, with the exception of its four stronger organizations, disbanded. The National League would, from 1892 through 1899, be a twelve-team circuit with a monopoly on major league players. In effect, a baseball trust had been created. The owners, who had always been consumed with themselves, now became absolutely insufferable in their conceit and enjoyment of the power they wielded over their players, who were regarded as objects to be moved around at will and, after a time, capriciously thrown away without a thought about the years of service they had accumulated. In fact, Arthur Soden, owner of the Boston Beaneaters, said precisely this, without any embarrassment: "When a player ceases to be useful to me, I will release him." No complications here. It was all very straightforward and businesslike. With the Brotherhood dead and no other major league to force competitive bidding for their skills, the best baseball players in the country became a depressed proletariat, pure and simple. Financial retrenchment was easy under these circumstances, and all clubs immediately cut their payrolls 30–40 percent. While there was no official maximum salary, there was an unofficial ceiling of $2,400, with no payment going to any player who was ill or hurt.

In the tumultuous 1890 season, one of the former American Association clubs that shifted over to the National League won the pennant. Brooklyn, temporarily known as the "Bridegrooms" because of the number of its players who coincidentally got married about the same time, became the only team ever to win consecutive pennants in two different major leagues. Opposing the Bridegrooms in the World Series were the Louisville Colonels, champions of the reeling American Association. The Colonels, too, had a historic distinction: they were the only major league club ever to climb from last place to first over a single season's span. This was to be the last World Series between the National League and American Association, and it turned out to be less than a memorable way to end the once very exciting rivalry. After each club had won three games and tied one, and rainy weather had forced several postponements so that it was already the end of October, there wasn't sufficient interest to schedule an eighth game to bring the series to a conclusion. Besides, Brooklyn didn't seem to many to be a real National League team and Louisville couldn't convince baseball fans that it was good enough to be playing in a World Series in the first place.

In 1895, Andrew Freedman purchased the New York Giants. Freedman was a sharp but thoroughly unlikable character, operating in real estate, public works, and insurance with very close ties to the top echelon of Tammany Hall. He never had a strong feeling for the game and entered it only to make money. From the outset he created nothing but hard feelings among players, newspaper reporters, and his fellow National League owners. He even had a run-in with the hallowed "Father" Chadwick. Chadwick took exception to Freedman's decision to bar a critical reporter from the Giants' training camp. Freedman decided that Chadwick would have to pay, literally, for supporting his colleague. The National League had awarded Chadwick a lifetime pension of $500 a year for his enormous contribution to baseball through virtually all of its history. Freedman accused Chadwick of sponging off league charity, which was a complete and patent falsehood but a hurtful remark nevertheless. Chadwick felt obliged to respond, asserting that he accepted the pension as an honor, remained financially independent, and intended to continue to report baseball news without any constraints. Freedman then announced that he would not pay his share of the money that went toward Chadwick's pension.

Following the collapse of the Players' League, the old Giants, who had thrown in their lot with the Brotherhood's New York entry, rejoined their former club. From 1892 through 1894, the Giants finished eighth, fifth, and second consecutively in the National League's twelve-team monopoly circuit. In this last season, their good showing made them eligible for the new-style World Series called the Temple Cup Series, in which the top two teams played a best-of-seven-games play-off for an ornate $800 trophy offered by self-declared "sportsman" William C. Temple of Pittsburg. The first-place team, the Baltimore Orioles, had won the pennant by the fairly slim margin of three games, so the expectation was that the postseason championship series would be close. In fact, it wasn't. Speedballer Amos Rusie, the "Hoosier Thunderbolt," who had had a great year for the Giants with a 36–13 record and a league-leading 195 strikeouts, led his club to a four-game sweep of the mortified Orioles. But the next season, the year Freedman took over and unsettled the champion New Yorkers, the Giants slipped to ninth place. Although Rusie managed to win 22 games and again lead the league with 201 strikeouts, he was blamed by Freedman for "indifferent work" in his last game and docked $200, a good part of his paycheck, going into the cold winter. The consequence was that Rusie, a proud man, refused to sign with Freedman's Giants for the 1896 season until he was given back the $200. "Monte" Ward, attorney, represented him before the National League board of owners, but Freedman's right to control his players' income

was affirmed. However, Freedman soon became as un-
popular with his fellow owners as he was with his players,
and they changed their position on the matter. After Rusie
had held out for the entire 1896 season with Freedman stead-
fast in his refusal to return the $200 and offer more than a
$2,400 contract, the other National League owners—not
known for their generosity toward their own players—decided to pool some of their own money and settle the issue.
The Rusie affair was getting out of hand in New York, and
this was of great importance to the National League owners
because of the city's stature and press coverage. Noel Hynd,
in his history of the Giants at the Polo Grounds, asserts that
whereas "New York fans merely hated Freedman" before he
went after their pitching ace,

> now they were ready to lynch him. That simple state-
> ment is barely an exaggeration. During the 1896 sea-
> son, a group of stockbrokers on Wall Street hung a
> sign out of their office windows urging a boycott of
> Giants' games until Rusie was paid and restored. A
> huge crowd gathered, shouting its approval and sug-
> gesting violence upon Freedman. Police had to forci-
> bly break up a near riot.

In 1897, Rusie returned to the field with a league-gathered
salary of $5,000 to make up for the year he missed and the
fine he was forced to pay at the conclusion of the 1894
season. The Rusie affair was typical of the confusion and
animosity Freedman injected whenever he touched any part
of the game.

As long as Freedman owned the Giants, they would be a
poor team, and, perversely, that was the way he intended to
keep it. Freedman was convinced that the twelve-team National League was just too big. "I will not attempt to improve
the New York club until the circuit is reduced," he said many
times. In addition, he wanted the neighboring Brooklyn

team out. Freedman's counterpart on the other side of the Brooklyn Bridge was Charley Ebbets. He had been with the Dodgers in one capacity or another from their early days, taking responsibility for all the little details around the park and office. The young Ebbets would sell tickets before the game and scorecards during the game, clean up after the game, and keep the books on days when there was no game; and when the opportunity arose, he purchased stock. By 1897, Ebbets was club president and part owner. On January 1, 1898, the formerly independent city of Brooklyn joined Manhattan in the creation of "Greater New York." Therefore, officially, there were two National League clubs in one city, and, simply put, Freedman wanted this city to himself.

Contrary to their staunch conviction, imperious personalities cannot always compel events to follow the direction they insist upon. Freedman decided that the Brooklyn club had to go so that his club could own Greater New York. But the Dodger directors refused to cooperate in their own demise. Instead, they went ahead and made a deal that, for a brief period of time, gave them the bragging rights to Greater New York and, in fact, the top spot in the National League. Brooklyn was involved in two mergers in 1898: one, an urban partnership with Manhattan; the other, a baseball partnership with the Baltimore Orioles, winners of the National League pennant in 1894, 1895, and 1896 and second-place finishers in 1897 and 1898. The owners of the Brooklyn and Baltimore clubs, following the "pooling" style of monopoly business in many other areas of the American economy, joined in what was called a "syndicate." Since, as a market, Brooklyn offered the greater potential for profits, the decision was made to shift Edward "Foxy Ned" Hanlon and a number of his stars from the Oriole to the Dodger roster. This was going to be a good team, and, it was decided, it should have a new identity befitting its high quality. It just so happened that there was a talented acrobatic act named

"Hanlon's Superbas" on the vaudeville circuit at the time. Since "Superbas" meant "the proud ones" and the new manager of the much-improved Brooklyn team was named Hanlon, the designation seemed absolutely inspired. Beginning with the 1899 season, the Brooklyn Superbas would take the field in a new Washington Park, at First Street and Third Avenue, catty-cornered across the intersection from the old one. In 1899 and 1900, the new Brooklyn Superbas won the National League pennant, while Freedman's bedraggled New York Giants finished tenth and eighth— eighth was last place in the pared-down circuit. Freedman's idea of a smaller National League had finally won out, but his last place finish within the eight-team operation certainly mocked his exceedingly bloated sense of what the world owed him.

During this last decade of the nineteenth century, a number of changes had taken place on the field of play. In 1893, two important provisions became permanent features of the game. First, the "infield-fly rule" was introduced to keep the defense from turning a fair pop-up in the area of the infield, with runners on first and second or first, second, and third and less than two outs, into a cheap double or triple play. Since the hitter is automatically called out under these circumstances, the runners are not in jeopardy—although they can put themselves in jeopardy if they decide to advance. Second, the pitching distance was moved back to sixty feet six inches and a twelve- by four-inch slab of rubber replaced the old pitching box as the marker. Ever since 1881, the pitcher looked at a hitter who, officially, was fifty feet away. But, since the 1886 regulation forced this pitcher to maintain contact with the back line of the five and a half-foot-long pitching box until he released the ball, the hitter was actually fifty-five feet six inches from the pitcher's anchored pivot foot. In effect, the National Rules Committee was simply and neatly moving the pitcher back five feet and erasing all but the back line of the pitching box. That old story about the odd six inches in the pitching distance being the result of a surveyor's misreading of a 6 for a 0 is satisfying for those of us who like to think that the "little guy" can suddenly intrude on haughty officialdom and contribute to history in unexpected ways, but it doesn't seem to be the case in this instance. Another story about this final change in the pitching distance might be true. The man who is usually singled out as being most responsible for the decision to go ahead with the shift backward as a safety precaution for National League hitters is Amos Rusie, the flame thrower whom Andrew Freedman nearly drove out of baseball. Finally, when pitchers in the opening games of the 1900 season faced home to throw their warm-up tosses, they no longer saw a corner of the angled diamond sheet of iron beneath the strike zone. Now, for the first time, home plate was a pentagon with the point facing backward and straight lines providing a better guide for those "corner" pitches that might force a hitter to make poor contact with the ball.

As the twentieth century began, the rules of the game were, for the most part, what they are today. However, the National League remained the only major league. Having fought off the Players' League, inherited the stronger elements of the defunct American Association, and suffered no competition at all since 1892, the National League-dominated baseball world appeared to be fixed—immutable, even.

2.

Real Men Don't Forgive

W hat the owners of the National League clubs of the 1890s, in their monopolistic complacency, did not anticipate was the emergence of someone even tougher, shrewder, and more resourceful than they were. Just short of 6 feet tall, moderately husky, hair parted right down the middle, bespectacled, his long face normally featuring an intimidating knitted brow and a somber downturn of the mouth, Byron Bancroft "Ban" Johnson, son of two very idealistic Ohio Protestant educators, was a model of the combattant who always triumphs because winning is simply essential to his constitution. He had been an able catcher at Oberlin and Marietta colleges—although he graduated from neither— and, as the sports editor of Cincinnati's *Commercial-Gazette*, he was used to blasting away at his carefully targeted enemies with unshakable conviction. Many saw in him the spirit of the premier achiever of the day, President Theodore Roosevelt. "Far better it is," said the spiritual leader of the Spanish-American War Rough Riders, "to dare mighty things, to win glorious triumphs, even though checkered by failure, than to rank with those poor spirits who neither enjoy nor suffer much, because they live in the gray twilight that knows not victory nor defeat."

In 1893, Charley Comiskey, player-manager of the Cincinnati Reds of the National League, recommended Johnson to the owners of the Western League as someone who might be able to save the failing minor circuit. Johnson took the job and by the end of the next season, in the midst of what was the worst economic depression America had suffered to date, seven of the eight clubs had already moved into the black. Johnson's prescription was sound finances, support for good umpires, and cleanly played baseball. By 1901, the Western had been renamed the American League, and it had boldly declared itself a major circuit. The established National League attempted to strike it down, but Ban Johnson had taken care to prepare the ground upon which his American League would stand and battle. Not only did he secure franchises in long-time baseball cities such as Chicago, Cleveland, Boston, Philadelphia, Baltimore, and Washington, but of the 182 players appearing on American League rosters in that initial year, 111 were former major leaguers with National League experience. "To bring the American League into being called for steeled resolution and courage in challenging a powerful, entrenched foe to war without quarter, with financial ruin as the penalty for defeat," remarks historian Allison Danzig pointedly. Johnson was the perfect man for the job; he could no more deny excitement to his blood than oxygen to his lungs.

For sure, the major weapon in Johnson's arsenal was that group of 111 ex-National Leaguers. The acquisition of these players began in 1900, when the Players Protective Association was founded. At the very end of the year, this association met with a committee of National League owners and presented its demands: an end to "farming" or the transfer of a major league player to the minors, an end to player sales without consent, and a five-year limitation on the reserve clause. At this point, the National League was still the only major league, and it was not about to take the time to deal seriously with these uppity player representatives. Ban Johnson had no love for unions either, but he recognized the value of winning over the Players Protective Association. At this point, Johnson was preparing to move franchises into Philadelphia, Boston, Washington, and Baltimore. To challenge the National League, his clubs would need established players, and a friendly Players Protective Association would help immensely in gaining their confidence. Charley "Chief" Zimmer, long time catcher for the Cleveland Spiders and now the Pittsburg Pirates, was the association's president. He and Hughie Jennings, former Baltimore Oriole shortstop who had just been sold by the Brooklyn Superbas to the Philadelphia Phillies, visited Johnson at the Lafayette Hotel in Philadelphia. "They wanted to know if he would agree in our contracts not to farm, or sell players without the players' consent," Johnson recalled. "Of course, I agreed to this. After expressing their friendliness to the American League, they took their departure." The way was clear for a mass defection away from the penny-pinching and insufferable arrogance of the National League owners. What had been heard was the opening salvo of what was soon to be called the "Great Baseball War."

Professional baseball, before television contracts, depended upon fan attendance, the "gate." "Kranks," as local loyalists were called in those days, paid the bills and provided the profits. In the first year of the "Great Baseball War," the National League edged the American League in drawing kranks, 1,920,031 to 1,683,584. But these were exceedingly impressive numbers for Johnson's brand-new major league, and National League owners were shaken. The following year, the American League outdrew the National 2,206,457 to

1,683,012. Another strong push and the "senior circuit" might drop back to a distinctly junior position—and Johnson knew precisely where to push.

When, in 1895, the infamous real estate tycoon Andrew Freedman took control of the New York Giants, he meant to insure his investment by keeping major league baseball on the island of Manhattan to himself. His control of leases on possible ballpark sites and his close friendship with Tammany Hall's Democratic Party boss Richard Croker—he had been best man at Croker's wedding—assured him a say in who did and did not play ball in New York. Therefore, when Ban Johnson made it clear that he was working to place an American League team in Manhattan, he was told, "No matter where you go, the City will decide to run a street car over second base." And, in late 1902, when it seemed as though a field-size lot on Lenox Avenue between 142nd and 144th Streets was available, the Freedman forces dashed American League hopes by preventing the closing of 143rd Street. It was imperative that Johnson play "political hard ball" if he was ever going to be permitted to play American League hard ball in New York. To do this he had to operate on the inside. The two insiders whom Johnson tactically chose as owners of the New York American League franchise were Frank Farrell and "Big Bill" Devery. Farrell had made his fortune as head of a syndicate that ran close to 250 horse race betting establishments. He had, in fact, been named by future District Attorney William T. Jerome as the major figure in the infamous New York gambling trust. Farrell's financial position was evident in the palace that served as his headquarters. The celebrated architect Stanford White had done the remodeling, at a cost of $500,000, of this "House with the Bronze Door," so called because of its massive Italian Renaissance entrance.

Devery's career was equally colorful. He went from bartender to the police force with the aid of his Tammany Hall connections and managed to stay "on the job" despite numerous and valid charges of corruption. The 1894 state Lexow Committee hearings found that Captain Devery's precinct was a cesspool of vice and corruption. It was Devery's philosophy, asserts Virgil W. Peterson, historian of organized crime in New York, "that people wanted vice, gambling, and liquor, and that it was the prerogative of the police to tolerate vice and share handsomely in the profits." In 1898, Devery made it to the top, being named chief of police by Tammany Mayor Robert A. Van Wyck. But, in 1901, the state legislature managed to throw Devery out by abolishing his office. Not one to give up easily, Devery got his Tammany friends to work on the problem, and before long, "Big Bill" regained full control over the force as Van Wyck's deputy police commissioner.

With the kind of local clout Farrell and Devery possessed, it was obvious to National League owners that they could not keep the door to New York baseball shut any longer and it seemed just as likely that they would have to conceive of a future that included the American League as a whole. Efforts to establish peaceful relations between the two leagues soon began to be exerted, especially after an incident that convinced Frank Robison, St. Louis Cardinal owner, that there were no more battlefields upon which to wage war. Robison was on his way to New York by train to attend a National League meeting when he saw that he was sharing a compartment with Charles Somers. Somers was a coal and shipping industrialist from Cleveland who personally funded the construction of American League ballparks in Boston and Philadelphia, helped the White Sox get established in Chicago, and owned the Cleveland franchise himself. Somers' contribution to American League baseball was estimated to be close to $5 million. "Ban Johnson built the American League," explains Johnson's biographer Eugene Murdock, "but Charles Somers paid the bills." On the train to New

York, Somers convinced Robison that the New York American League club had solved its ballpark site problem—which was not quite the truth. Robison decided that the time was right to make a move that would be good for baseball as a whole. When he got to the National League gathering at the Victoria Hotel, he successfully lobbied for the formation of a committee "for the purpose of conferring with representatives of the America League . . . to ascertain upon what basis . . . [peace] can be accomplished." On December 12, 1902, Ban Johnson met with the members of this committee and told them that the American League welcomed peace talks. An interleague conference was the next step, and this took place in Cincinnati on January 9, 1903. There, differences were resolved regarding contracts, territorial claims, and disputed player ownership. A resolution was passed, disallowing any further league jumping.

When the National League ratification meeting was held, also in Cincinnati, on January 19, only one man swam against the tide, John Tomlinson Brush, the new owner of the New York Giants. Born in Clintonville, New York, in 1845, Brush was quickly introduced to the harsher side of life, being orphaned at four and moved, along with his brother and two sisters, to his grandparents' tiny rural home, where, because of space problems, he and his brother George had to live in an unheated barn. In 1863, Brush enlisted in the 1st New York Artillery and served until the Civil War's end. After military service, he clerked in several stores, gaining experience and enough money to invest in his own clothing establishment in Indianapolis, Indiana. His flair for commerce was clear from the outset. Having waited much too long, in his estimation, for the construction of the building that was to house his great venture, he hit upon an idea that would not only hasten the masons but prepare the way for customers. His daughter, Natalie Brush de Gendron, tells the story:

My father took a full page ad in the newspapers with only the word "WHEN" printed on the page. He rented the roofs and barns all over the state and had "WHEN" painted on them and he emblazoned "WHEN" over the front of the still abuilding store. Naturally, curiosity was aroused. By the time of the opening everybody knew the "WHEN" store and that was the name which was retained.

Brush's entry into the world of baseball ownership was prompted by the opportunity it offered to promote his clothing business. By 1887, he was the forty-two-year-old owner of the Indianapolis Indians, one of the weaker franchises in the National League. In 1890, Brush sacrificed his operation to rebuild the New York Giants, a club devastated by defections to the Players' League, a circuit organized by the ballplayers themselves in protest of the unfair contractual arrangements and financial conditions in the National League and American Association. At the conclusion of the season, with the Players' League now defunct, Brush was rewarded for his efforts to save the New York ball club with the new National League franchise in Cincinnati. The decision was somewhat controversial because Cleveland streetcar owner Albert Johnson had been led to believe that *he* would be awarded the franchise and had already leased a playing field for the following season. The sports editor of the Cincinnati *Commercial-Gazette*, twenty-six-year-old Ban Johnson, was a close friend—not a relative—of Albert, and blasted Brush whenever he had the opportunity. Because Brush directed his Cincinnati club from Indianapolis, Ban Johnson accused him of being a careless absentee owner and charged that he was a bad influence on baseball. So much grief did Johnson give Brush that his press pass was taken away. "From that time the sporting editor had to pay to get in," relates Eugene Murdock. "Having no desk to write on, he brought a clipboard with him. As the fans learned what had happened, they would crowd around the writer and urge him to lay it on Brush."

The paths of the two headstrong ascending figures, Johnson and Brush, crossed once again when Johnson assumed the presidency of the Western League. Sure enough, as the new director began his amazing resurrection of the dying Western League, there was Brush, owner of the Indianapolis team, ready to vex him. Brush engaged in a practice that came to be named after him, "Brushism." It had to do with the system of drafting and farming players. Major league teams were allowed to take players from the minors at fixed prices. If a drafted player did not perform up to expectations, he could be farmed back down to any minor league team. The big loser in this arrangement was the strong minor league team that lost key players in the major league draft only to find them redirected to a competing organization. Such a pattern was a regular occurrence in Ban Johnson's Western League, with John Brush's major league Cincinnati club drafting many of the circuit's stars, and his minor league club receiving a large number of those same players. In 1895, the first year of "Brushism," one writer observed that "Brush was switching players back and forth so frequently that the Western League Club should be called 'Cincinnapolis.' By mid-season nine Cincinnati players had been sent down to Indianapolis which explained why the Hoosiers rose so rapidly in the standings." Indianapolis won the Western League pennant three times and came in second twice in the next five years. As Murdock states, "Johnson was not the only Western League official who was hostile to Brush. Every owner in the league resented the man. Brush, for his part, did not propose to let any crowd of minor leaguers push him around."

In spite of the animosity between Brush and Johnson, in January 1903, Brush's fellow National League owners asked him to accept Ban Johnson's American League with a New

York organization in Manhattan included. This request not only caused excruciating pain in the old personal wounds that remained gaping, but threatened to rob him of his paying customers. Brush desperately fought back. He sought legally to enjoin his colleagues from signing a compact with Johnson, but his attempts failed. He inspired a petition among Washington Heights property owners that asked the District Governing Board to deny the American League a playing field on 165th Street, but this action, too, failed. Finally, the bitter but temporarily spent Giant owner sullenly withdrew his opposition to the peace agreement between the two major leagues so that the endorsement of the ratification statement could be unanimous. A new era in professional baseball had begun, but Brush would not remain inactive if an opportunity arose for him to strike a return blow.

Brush did not look like a man carrying a great hatred. Thin with thin features in an age of bloated bellies and faces, his only striking feature was his mustache, which mimicked his name exceedingly well. In a confrontation with Ban Johnson, he seemed physically overwhelmed. However, Brush would not have to wage his battle against Johnson alone. He would be joined by one of the most notorious, contentious, venomous brawlers of this belligerent era: John Joseph McGraw—the man called "Little Napoleon." McGraw had fought his way up from a poor and tragic childhood in Truxton, (central) New York, and struggled through an early baseball career of only modest success. McGraw's father was an unskilled laborer who managed to support his large family, nine children, by repairing railroad tracks. In the winter of 1884–1885, diptheria struck Truxton, and John, the eldest boy at eleven years of age, lost his mother, two sisters, and two brothers within a period of a few weeks.

Although his father strongly disapproved, John decided to test his ability to earn a living playing baseball in the low minor leagues. It was not until he traveled to Cuba on a

barnstorming tour that he competed against quality profes-
sionals. Back in the United States, McGraw stood out at
shortstop against the National League Cleveland Spiders in
an early season exhibition game. Another exhibition contest
against Adrian "Cap" Anson's Chicago White Stockings
gained him additional attention, especially as he brazenly
taunted the famous manager-first baseman. By the middle of
the year 1891, McGraw was asked to join the American
Association Baltimore Orioles, a major league team. For the
next few seasons, when the Orioles shifted over to the National League, McGraw performed competently in the infield
and outfield. By 1894, he began to make his mark as the
regular third baseman. Things never came easily or naturally
to the smallish 5-foot-7, 155-pound McGraw, so he learned
that scrupulous planning, hard work, and an iron will were
the means required to reach his goals. He also benefited
greatly from a harsh view of the baseball field as a jungle
where survival depended upon a lethally aggressive approach at all times. McGraw always pressed the action for
fear that a single moment of relaxation would cost him the
victory he so badly needed. "Baseball always took too much
out of me," he said of the sport others presumed he loved. "It
always hashed my nerves and unstrung me so that I wasn't
fit to be seen or heard. . . . In playing or managing, the game
of ball is only fun for me when I'm out in front and winning.
I don't care a bag of peanuts for the rest of the game."
Blanche McGraw, John's wife of thirty-two years, saw him as
"a force that knew only one compromise: victory. All else was
of minor importance. . . ." Over and over again, through the
hundreds of anecdotes produced by a major league career of
forty-one bruising and raucous years, a single curt and intimidating message could be heard: "The main idea is to win."

McGraw learned to win with the legendary Orioles of the
mid-1890s, "the swashbuckling knights of the baseball trails."
The whole notorious bunch of them, it was said, "break-

fasted on gunpowder and warm blood." In his first game in the National League, the great Honus Wagner experienced the Oriole treatment: "On my first time up, I got a single. The next time I might have had a triple but Jack Doyle gave me the hip at first, Hughie Jennings chased me wide around second, and John McGraw blocked me off at third, then jammed the ball into my belly, knocking the wind out of me." Umpires, too, had to be wary. John Heydler, president of the National League from 1918 to 1934 and an umpire in the 1890s, had very bitter memories of McGraw and company:

> They were mean, vicious, ready at any time to maim a rival player or an umpire if it helped their cause. The things they would say to an umpire were unbelievably vile, and they broke the spirits of some fine men. I've seen umpires bathe their feet by the hour after McGraw and others spiked them through their shoes. The club was never a constructive force in the game. The worst of it was, they got by with much of their brow beating and hooliganism. Other clubs patterned after them, and I feel the lot of the umpire was never worse than in the years when the Orioles were flying high.

But it was not just nastiness that the Orioles brought to the game. They used a special kind of intelligence, also. "Inside baseball" was what people called it. This was a studied effort to work all the angles of all the rules and possibilities of a given situation. The bunt, hit-and-run, and "Baltimore chop" were its weapons. "Take the bunt," Oriole catcher Wilbert Robinson asserted.

> It may have been seen occasionally somewhere before, but if so it made no lasting impression. The first men to realize its practical value were ["Wee Willie"] Keeler and McGraw. Both were fast runners. Dumping the ball was an astounding thing to players of those days. Unprepared as the third and first base-

men were for a thing like that, before they could handle the ball, fleet Keeler or McGraw were across the base, kidding the other fellows.

Singles, steals, and spikes were the Oriole trademarks. They played hard and, as they loved to brag, they played hurt. "We'd spit tobacco juice on a spike wound, rub dirt in it, and get out there and play," claimed McGraw.

McGraw's route to New York was tortuous, noisy, and littered with ill will. When, in 1898, Baltimore owners Harry von der Horst and Ned Hanlon (also president and manager) formed a syndicate with Brooklyn's principal owner Ferdinand Abell, the direction of both clubs was openly merged. Since Brooklyn offered a greater potential for profits, the decision was made to move Hanlon and a number of his stars from Baltimore. It was arranged for McGraw to stay in Baltimore and manage what remained of that club. Unfortunately, in the following year, 1900, the National League cut back from twelve to eight teams, and Baltimore was one of those abandoned. McGraw now saw his future in terms of managing, and his vision was appreciated by Hanlon, who sold his contract to St. Louis, where Cardinal owner Frank DeHaas Robison offered McGraw the position of player-manager. But the former Oriole would accept only a one-year player's agreement. In Baltimore, near his Diamond Café business, was where he wanted to be, and there seemed to be a new and promising way to return. Ban Johnson's American League was going major in 1901, and he wanted a Baltimore franchise. In October, McGraw and his pal Wilbert Robinson, who also played in St. Louis in 1900, met with Johnson in Chicago. There McGraw was offered the position of manager of the proposed Baltimore organization, which was to carry the Oriole name into the American League future. However, Ban's agreement with McGraw, the man who bore a reputation for extreme rowdiness, was *not* without stipulation. He told McGraw, "I am going to run the American League as a clean league. Clean baseball will be one of the platforms we will wage our fight on. Many things have been going on in the National League that have disgusted patrons of the game. These things must stop. Furthermore, as a league president, I always back up my umpires. Now, I know of your reputation in the National League; you're a battler, and you've made it very tough for Nick Young's [National League president, 1885–1902] umpires."

"I always play hard, and play to win," explained McGraw. "That also is the way I run my teams."

"Yes, John," responded Johnson, "I know you are an aggressive ball player and manager, and of your intense desire to win. I don't want to curb your zeal; it is desirable in a baseball man, but aggressiveness cannot be carried into rowdyism. You must understand now I will tolerate no rough stuff, nor the type of language you and your Oriole players have used in the past."

"I think we can get along," said McGraw, as the interview ended.

It was up to McGraw, as manager, to go out and get some ballplayers for his new team. Since this was its first year of major league competition, the American League, if it was to reach the highest of playing standards, had to entice established stars away from the rival National League. "Raiding" is the appropriate term for what was done, and McGraw was one of Johnson's primary raiders. The objective was not to steal National Leaguers under contract for the year 1901, but to convince those who had not yet signed a contract to ignore the reserve clause. The most convincing argument McGraw and the other American League raiders presented for jumping was the opportunity to earn more money. Typical was the case of "Iron Man" Joe McGinnity, the strong-armed right-hander out of Rock Island, Illinois. Joe needed the money he got as a ballplayer. His off-season occupation as an iron-worker—the source of his nickname—did not provide much in the way of financial security. In 1899, his rookie season, McGinnity had proven himself to be valuable property by winning 28 games (losing 17) for McGraw's Orioles. This mark earned him a tie for the league lead with Jim Hughes of Brooklyn. The next year, McGinnity joined Hughes as the Baltimore-Brooklyn syndicate transferred the promising young pitcher to the pennant-winning Superbas. That his first year was no fluke was clear to all who saw him perform in 1900. By season's end, he recorded the best totals in three major categories: wins, with 29 (losing just 9); games pitched, with 45; and innings pitched, with 347. A prospect such as this, one would imagine, would be weighed down with money so that he could not jump anywhere. But this was not the case. McGraw met his former and future ace in February 1901 in the cold waiting room of St. Louis' Union Station. "The money good, Mac?" asked McGinnity. "Good as gold, Joe," answered McGraw. "Every penny." "Placing the contract on his knee, and the pen in his rough and grubby hand," wrote Blanche McGraw, "the greatest of all curve-ball pitchers signed to play for the Baltimore Orioles of the American League. . . ."

Ban Johnson intended to win the competition between his American League and the old National League. To do this he was determined to present a better, more acceptable brand of baseball. "CLEAN BALL is the MAIN PLANK in the American League platform," began his first bulletin to club owners,

> and the clubs must stand by it religiously. There must be no profanity on the ball field. The umpires are agents of the League and must be treated with re-spect. I will suspend any manager or player who uses profane or vulgar language to an umpire, and that

suspension will remain in force until such time as the offender can learn to bridle his tongue. Rowdyism and profanity have worked untold injury to baseball. To permit it would blight the future of the American League. This bulletin you will please hand to your manager so that he may impart its content to the players.

The message must have caused McGraw, one of the most ferocious umpire baiters in the history of the game, at least a moment's concern. But this moment seems to have passed quickly because early in the season, in Boston, McGraw gave American League kranks a scene from one of his famous acts. Umpire John Haskell made a decision McGraw did not care for, and he let him know it by cursing him, pushing him, and jumping up and down on the staggered arbiter's toes. Haskell recovered his senses and threw the sputtering McGraw out of the game; whereupon, Johnson, true to bulletin number one, suspended the Oriole leader for five days. During the course of the 1901 season, there were many other disciplinary actions merited by McGraw and his team, including a suspension issued in September for the remainder of the year handed to Joe McGinnity for cursing, shoving, and spraying an umpire with tobacco juice. "This League will not stand for such tactics," Johnson reminded McGraw. "Early in the season, you received my bulletin on conduct on the field. I took it up with you personally, item for item. Now, I must warn you, in all solemnity, that your misconduct, and that of your players, must stop." "Your umpires are always picking on me, and my team," replied McGraw. "They always have rabbit ears when they umpire Oriole games. Why don't they hear some of the things other teams are saying about them?"

On opening day, 1902, McGraw was thrown out for abusive language. Within a week, he was accused of inciting Baltimore fans to attack umpire Jack Sheridan, and Johnson suspended him for five days. At the end of June, the Orioles were playing Boston and had an important rally going in the seventh inning. But the momentum was abruptly halted when umpire Tommy Connolly called Baltimore right fielder Cy Seymour out for failing to touch third base. McGraw went wild, was ordered off the field, refused to leave, and provoked Connolly into forfeiting the game. The next day, Ban Johnson sent McGraw a wire: "As of today, you are suspended indefinitely." A month before, McGraw had had a costly run-in with Detroit outfielder Dick Harley. "There was a feud on between McGraw and Harley," veteran reporter Jim Price remembered.

> McGraw had a sharp tongue, and could get under the skins of his opponents with his barbed taunts. Harley seemed to be smarting over something McGraw had said to him earlier in the game, and there is no doubt in my mind that he was out to get John. He came in with his spikes high and kicked out with one foot as he approached McGraw.

The result was three extremely deep gashes on the left leg, just below the kneecap. McGraw never fully recovered from this spiking. Spitting tobacco juice and rubbing dirt on it did not allow him to "get out there and play" this time. He would not have a serious, active role in the few years into which he attempted to stretch his playing career. He could, however, continue managing if he could find a ball club that wanted him. The question was, could he stay in his favored Baltimore or anywhere else in the American League while Ban Johnson was president?

Through much of 1902, Johnson and McGraw were involved in more than a battle over the sanctity of the decisions of umpires. Johnson wanted and needed an American League team in New York, and he had settled on Baltimore as the franchise to be moved. McGraw made several trips to

New York to make preliminary arrangements for this bold invasion of National League turf. In fact, while McGraw was convalescing from the Harley spiking, he visited New York and met with Frank Farrell on the matter of acquiring a plot of land for a playing field. Johnson, according to sportswriter Frank Menke, had previously told McGraw that he would be in charge of the team to be transferred from Baltimore to New York. But McGraw's habitual ball field tantrums and physical abuse of umpires caused a fast deterioration in his relationship with Johnson. Besides, McGraw's record as a manager was far from impressive. His 1899 National League Orioles finished fourth; his 1901 American League Orioles finished fifth; and his 1902 club was also heading to a second division finish. It seems likely, as the very knowledgeable sportswriter Fred Lieb believed, that during McGraw's indefinite suspension, he was advised that "he no longer was being considered in the future of New York American League picture." It was at this juncture that events of consequence began to take place—and swiftly. Andrew Freedman, owner of the New York Giants, had spoken to McGraw when the latter visited New York as Johnson's special agent. Now he decided to take advantage of the deepening hostility between McGraw and Johnson by making a job offer that might well help the Giants and definitely rock the upstart and much too successful American League. Freedman sent his secretary, Fred Knowles, to Baltimore to ask McGraw if he would be interested in managing the Giants. If he said yes, Knowles was prepared to hand over a four-year agreement, calling for a huge salary of $11,000 a year and a guarantee of supreme authority over all baseball matters. McGraw wanted to accept these very generous terms and get away from Ban Johnson, but first he had to get out of his Baltimore contract. The Orioles, McGraw later divulged, were losing money, and he had advanced between $6,000 and $7,000 to pay player salaries:

I called a meeting of the directors and put the matter squarely up to them. "Gentlemen, here is the situation," I told them. "I have advanced nearly $7,000 to keep the club going. The company is in debt to me that much personally. Now, I think I should be paid that money back or I should be given my unconditional release. It's not up to me to carry the club. We've got to have a showdown. You can do either one thing or the other."

We discussed the matter at length but nobody seemed willing to reimburse me for what I had paid out. At the end of the discussion it was decided to give me my unconditional release. That was done. I was free to do as I pleased.

On July 19, McGraw was pleased to formally take over command of the New York Giants. Years after, McGraw, "in a mellow mood," looked back at this critical period in his life. "Do you want to know why I left Baltimore, and the American League in 1902?" he asked Fred Lieb, the ubiquitous baseball journalist.

Well, I'll give you the real story. The move to shift the Orioles to New York had been contemplated for some time. In fact, I did much of the ground work, built up the contacts, scouted around for the grounds, and was to get a piece of the club. Naturally, I assumed I would be manager. Then I suddenly learned that I no longer figured in Johnson's New York plans and that he was preparing to ditch me at the end of the 1902 season. So I acted fast. If he planned to ditch me, I ditched him first, and beat him to New York by nearly a year.

"The things that most people remembered about McGraw," wrote biographer Joseph Durso, "were those steady blue eyes, that don't-tread-on-me toughness and the uncringing determination not to be left holding the bag."

When the McGraw story became public knowledge, the

entire baseball world was stunned. Johnson and other American Leaguers called him a "traitor, renegade, and Benedict Arnold." Before the cascade of names began, McGraw had assured Baltimore Oriole officials that he would not tamper with any of their players. But the heat coming from his former cohorts moved McGraw's chemistry to the point of explosion. Together with John T. Brush, chairman of the National League's Executive Committee, McGraw engineered a stock buying scheme that left Andrew Freedman with a majority interest in the Orioles. Now Freedman could shift players deemed worthy to the Giants or any other National League club, and he proceeded to do exactly this with six of the Orioles' best performers. Johnson was absolutely enraged. He believed, according to Murdock, that "this was a deliberate plan to wreck the American League." Henceforth, the enmity between Johnson and McGraw reached and remained epic in its dimensions. It was regarded as baseball's number one hatred.

In the fall of 1902, Andrew Freedman, whose primary interest had become helping to finance the construction of New York's first subway, the Interborough Rapid Transit (IRT) system, sold the Giants to John T. Brush for $200,000. Brush got the money for this purchase by selling his Cincinnati Reds to the Fleishmann brothers, Julius and Max, for $150,000 and making the unusual arrangement to borrow the rest from other National League owners. Would the tight-fisted and puritanical Brush pay the bills needed to rebuild the Giants and tolerate the near-hysterical antics of his ultra-aggressive new manager? After all, it was Brush who, in 1888, authored the "Classification Plan," which would have grouped players according to their "habits, earnestness, and special qualifications" and paid them accordingly and little; and it was Brush who, in 1898, devised the "Purification Plan," which aimed at eliminating "obscene, indecent, or vulgar language" by allowing anyone—fans included—to report gross incivilities to a board of discipline empowered to suspend or even ban a player or manager.

As the 1903 season wore on, it was evident that whatever restrictive financial and ethical standards Brush had set in the past, he was going to leave McGraw alone to guide the Giants to baseball respectability. "He was heart and soul with me in my plan to build a club," recalled McGraw with satisfaction.

> He didn't care what players I bought or what I paid for them as long as my judgment dictated their purchase. Right here I would like to say that not once from then until his death did Mr. Brush ever interfere with me in the slightest way. He gave me the reins and told me to go just as far as I liked.

So, a partnership was formed. Brush and McGraw, two rural New Yorkers with iron wills forged in the intense heat of damaged childhoods, with the proclivity for nervy strategies, and with the habit of seeing every challenge in personal terms and in crisis dimensions, were fixed with total resolution on the goal of winning the championship. However, this was much harder to accomplish now. The best in the National League had to defeat the best in Ban Johnson's American League in a postseason series to be the World Champs. What greater personal joy could both Brush and McGraw have than to beat a team wearing the colors of Ban Johnson's American League? On the other hand, if things went wrong, what could be a greater calamity?

3.

Who Owns
New York?

A ll too often the weather seems deliberately to
ridicule our grand ordering of events. Although January 1, 1898, was scheduled to be
an altogether new and glorious day in the life of New Yorkers, the evening before was marked by a heavy, drenching
mixture of rain and snow. Nevertheless, a mass of people
continued to gather at Union Square on Fourteenth Street,
prepared to march down Broadway to City Hall, set aglow by
500 magnesium lights, in order to celebrate the first moment
of "Greater New York." Up to this point, the city of New York
consisted of the island of Manhattan and southern town-
ships in Westchester County known as the Bronx. From
January 1, 1898, it would also consist of the formerly independent city of Brooklyn and the many villages of Queens
and Richmond (or Staten Island). As midnight neared, the
crowd of 100,000 assembled between Broadway and Park
Row stared intently at the roof line of the badly neglected
eighty-six-year-old French Renaissance-Georgian style City

Hall that would now serve as the governmental center of a metropolis stretching across 320 square miles and containing 3.4 million citizens. Chicago included 1.7 million people and, therefore, no longer threatened New York's claim as the greatest city in the country. James Phelan, mayor of San Francisco, 3,250 miles away, pressed a button launching an electric impulse that crossed the country and ran right up the staff attached to City Hall's cupola, smartly raising the new blue and white flag of Greater New York.

Even before the proclamation of Greater New York, it was generally recognized that the horse-drawn streetcars that moved New Yorkers around were not efficient enough for a rapidly growing city of serious scale. In 1875, the Board of Rapid Transit Commissioners decided that the construction of elevated railways was the answer and that Second, Third, Sixth, and Ninth avenues were the right sites. Coal-burning locomotives were to power these steam engines along tracks hoisted two stories over the clogged streets of Manhattan by closely-spaced supporting piers. The "Elevateds" or "Els" were certainly an improvement in terms of transit, but there was a price to pay. A blanket of soot fell everywhere. The pounding noise of the engine and the screeching of breaks on iron rail could be absolutely deafening. And the hot coal embers that dropped onto awnings caused fires. By 1903, much of the health and fire hazards and filth of the coal-burning locomotives were eliminated when the El engines were converted to electricity, but there was still the inescapable presence of the looming El itself and the deep shadows it cast. Areas alongside the El were awful places to reside and quickly became depressed.

New Yorkers going to the Polo Grounds to see the Giants had the option of the Sixth Avenue El, which cost $.05, or horsedrawn carriages, which charged $1.00 for the first mile, $.40 for each additional mile, and $.30–$.40 for every fifteen-minute waiting period. All games were concluded before dark in this era before lighted ball fields, so, regarding the weekdays, only those who could arrange their hours could get to the park by late afternoon. Starting time for most clubs was three o'clock or three-thirty calculating that since games were almost always completed within two hours, loyal rooters could expect to be home by dinner time. The Giants, however, did not start until four o'clock, allowing the Wall Street crowd a full hour to catch and travel on the Sixth Avenue El express.

The Sixth Avenue El began at Battery Place, at the southernmost point of Manhattan's West Side, and continued along West Broadway, where the Polo Grounds-bound businessmen climbed the two-story covered stairway to a station that could be as surprisingly elaborate as the one at Fourteenth Street, which earnestly tried to give the appearance of a Swiss Chalet.

The Lower West Side contained most of the city's historical, commercial, and official sites and buildings. Here was Battery Park, named for the cannon that guarded the island in the seventeenth century; the enormous Produce Exchange in dark red brick over one of the earliest iron-skeleton support structures, with a main hall on the second floor that measured 220 feet by 144 feet across and 60 feet to the skylight above; the Gothic Revival Trinity Church in its elegant third form since 1697, easily spotted by its towering 280-foot spire, the most conspicuous of Manhattan's landmarks for many years; the Subtreasury Building (now Federal Hall), site of the Stamp Act Congress, first capitol of the United States, and inauguration of President George Washington; the Neo-Classical Stock Exchange (a year old in 1904), whose 52½-foot Corinthian columns were a far cry from the simple buttonwood tree that marked Wall Street's first brokerage site; and the New York City Courthouse, whose outrageous cost, somewhere between $9 and $12 million, remained a constant reminder of the shameless thievery of Tammany

Hall Boss William Marcy Tweed and political corruption in general.

Across Broadway and Centre Street, just northeast of City Hall, was a very different New York. The sites here revealed no preserved history, charming aesthetics, or lavish expenditure. This was the four-square-mile Lower East Side, home of the newest and poorest immigrants. People lived here packed one thousand to an acre in tenements, one of which was grievously described by contemporary journalist Jacob Riis, in his classic *How the Other Half Lives:*

> The hall is dark and you might stumble over the children pitching pennies back there. Not that it would hurt them; kicks and cuffs are their daily diet. They have little else. . . . A flight of stairs. You can feel your way, if you cannot see it. Close? Yes! What would you have? All the fresh air that ever enters these stairs comes from the hall-door that is forever slamming, and from the windows of dark bedrooms that in turn receive from the stairs their sole supply of the elements God meant to be free, but man deals out with such a niggardly hand. . . . Here is a door. Listen! That short hacking cough, that tiny helpless wail—what do they mean? . . . Oh! a sadly familiar story—before the day is at an end. The child is dying of the measles. With half a chance it might have lived; but it had none. That dark bedroom killed it.

Aboard the green four-car Sixth Avenue El train, the Wall Streeters would proceed up West Broadway and then, after the Bleecker Street Station, shift over to Sixth Avenue itself. Beneath the El was Greenwich Village, rapidly populated in the early nineteenth century by New Yorkers moving northward to escape repeated outbreaks of smallpox and yellow fever. By 1811, the Village had so quickly been established that the Commissioners' Plan for Manhattan, with its projected grid pattern, had to begin further north at Houston Street. In the early twentieth century, the crooked streets and inexpensive rents appealed to avant–garde artists and writers, and, so, the Village became marked as New York's offbeat section.

Moving uptown, the train passed from Thirteenth Street to Twenty-third Street, right through the Sixth Avenue-Broadway area known as "Ladies Mile," blocks of department stores serving the needs of middle- to upper-class consumers. While the El had a decidedly damaging effect on residential areas, it made the Sixth Avenue emporia tremendously successful. Looking down on Fourteenth Street, El riders could spot the narrow Beaux-Arts structure anchoring the group of interconnected buildings belonging to R.H. Macy and Company, billed as the "world's largest store." Five–hundred red and black delivery wagons circulated throughout the city bringing Macy's goods to those unable or unwilling to use the El or surface transportation. Four blocks up, just below the Eighteenth Street El station, was Siegel-Cooper and Company. The suggestion to New Yorkers to "meet me at the fountain" meant a rendezvous on the large marble terrace of the six-story Siegel-Cooper store, which was centered around a white marble and brass statue of "The Republic," enclosed by colorfully illuminated jets of water. On Twentieth Street was the huge Hugh O'Neill store, whose giant white Renaissance towers rose high above a five-story façade of Corinthian columns and pilasters as well as the El. O'Neill had a reputation for taking a personal interest in his employees, giving them time off with pay for religious holidays—a gesture well-received by department store hands who generally worked a sixty-four-hour week.

At Twenty-third Street, a lateral move eastward would present the incomparable twenty-one story Flatiron Building, conceived by Daniel Burnham, the celebrated architect who was a principal designer of the very influential 1893 World's Columbian Exposition in Chicago and the restructured mall in Washington, D.C. Originally called the Fuller Building, after the construction company that built and owned it, its extremely odd triangular shape, conforming to the "flatiron block" upon which it was erected, forced a change in reference. At its narrowest end, at Twenty-third Street where Broadway and Fifth Avenue meet, what was for a brief time the world's tallest habitable building is only six feet wide. There the wind charged around both converging sides and issued a frightening howl into the ears of astonished passersby. "Pictured on postcards, stamped on souvenirs," notes *The W.P.A. Guide to New York,*

> its image was familiar to American minds, young and old. Standing on what was traditionally the windiest corner of the city, it was facetiously considered a good vantage point for the glimpse of a trim ankle, in the long-skirted, pre-war era; policemen used to shoo loungers away from the Twenty-third Street corner, and the expression "Twenty-three skidoo" is supposed to have originated with this association.

It was in this building that Ban Johnson located his eastern office. Ironically, just up Fifth Avenue, at Twenty-Seventh Street and in direct view of Johnson's office, was the Victoria Hotel, where John McGraw lived when he first came to New York, fleeing the soured relationship with Johnson that had developed in Baltimore.

From Madison Square, immediately beyond the Flatiron Building, north to the Forty-second Street area was New York's "Rialto," the famous "Great White Way" or theater district, where packed crowds gathered before giant marquees of lights advertising spectaculars on the way to selling out. The world-famous crossroads of Forty-second Street, Broadway, and Seventh Avenue, formerly known as Longacre Square, was, in 1904, renamed Times Square in honor of the twenty-five-story tower building that served as the new headquarters of *The New York Times,* long one of the most potent forces in the city's view of itself and the world.

To the east, along Fifth Avenue, were society's fabulous mansions. Here lived some of the richest people in America. "It is too evident that money cannot have much value here," commented French visitor Paul Bourget. "There is too much of it." Every morning Henry Osborne Havemeyer, the "Sugar King of the East," practiced his violin in a room where, as Fifth Avenue's historian Kate Simon describes it,

> the furniture . . . was light and delicate, set against oriental panels on subtly tinted wallpaper, a most tactful background for unique Chinese vases and rugs and oriental lacquers. Above, wondrous Tiffany chandeliers, cluster of bubbling glass of blossoms on slender branches of art nouveau metal. Tiffany devised, also, a suspended staircase of many frail elements, a fantasy from Arabian Nights. . . . The adjoining lamps were bold, eclectic—Carolingian crowns studded with glass, supports in Chinese curves, suggestions of the Moorish—unparalleled in their inventiveness and dramatic effect.

Could it be that these people lived in the same city—even on the same planet—as the tenement dwellers of the Lower East Side?

The El continued up Sixth Avenue to Fifty-third Street, where the tracks veered westward to Ninth Avenue, called Columbus Avenue above Fifty-ninth Street. As the train moved uptown, the visual story was Central Park to the east and the products of two decades of building boom on the Upper West Side. At Seventy-second Street and Central Park West was the Dakota, the first of the area's great apartment buildings, or "French flats"—a term used to dissociate respectable multifamily residences from the sordid impression of the tenements. When this fanciful, gable-roofed, ten-story structure with the yellow brick stone trim and terra cotta ornaments was completed in 1884, its numerous detractors snickered that it was so far north of civilization, "it might as well be in Dakota," furnishing it with a name. However, by 1904, there were many other French flats along and between Central Park West, Columbus Avenue, Amsterdam Avenue, and Broadway.

Central Park, the scenery a block away from the Sixth Avenue El, beginning at Fifty-ninth Street and ending at 110th Street, was a half-century old and, in itself, a remarkable success. However, its splendid lakes, hills, meadows, recreational facilities, sculptures, and zoo benefited only uptown and wealthier New Yorkers. It was four miles from the Lower East Side, whose residents were limited to their own immediate neighborhoods by the daily struggle for existence. As Otto Bettmann, founder of the fascinating New York print and photograph archive that bears his name, noted, "It was said that 'for the mass of people, the Park might have been 100 miles away, too distant even for an annual outing.' "

Across Central Park was the Upper East Side. Here, behind the climbing mansions of Fifth Avenue, was a slower development. The major impediment was the New York and Harlem Railroad, which was consolidated in 1863 with the New York Central. The railroad's right-of-way, lying in an open trench up and down Fourth Avenue, polluted much of the area with noxious smoke, soot, and noise. Aaron E. Klein, in his history of the New York Central, adds that the presence of the railroad was also

> a dangerous situation, and there were many accidents. The Central did not improve its relations with the locals by building a yard that extended north to 49th Street [from Grand Central Station on 42nd Street] and west to Madison Avenue. There was constant movement by switch engines in the yard, and anyone trying to cross the complex of tracks did so at his own peril. The situation became a grand case for newspapers. The general demand was for the Central

to sink the tracks below street level—an expensive undertaking which the Central was not too eager to begin.

When, in 1907, the New York Central was electrified and the Fourth Avenue trench covered, the Upper East Side quickly became a very desirable part of town, and rapid development began.

At 110th Street, the Sixth Avenue El turned right—abruptly—over a tall, rickety-looking support structure that swung north on Eighth Avenue (now Frederick Douglass Boulevard) through the village of Harlem. "Apartment houses were beginning to rise in Harlem, along Lenox, St. Nicholas and Seventh Avenues," explains New York City social historian Lloyd Morris.

But, mainly it was a community of small, middle-class homes, impeccably respectable, conservative and prosperous. On pleasant summer evenings, you saw families sitting out on their stoops, and children playing in streets seldom disturbed by traffic. You surmised that the aroma of well-cooked meals saturated the low brownstone dwellings. You could be sure that every parlor displayed an aspidistra, a "suite" of mahogany-stained furniture upholstered in velveteen, an upright piano and gilt-framed chromos and engravings on the walls. Upstairs, the principal bedroom would have a gleaming, knobby brass double bed, with cover and "pillowshams" of crochet lace over a lining of pink or blue sateen. In these homes, pinochle was played and pyrography cultivated as a genteel art. As you walked past them you heard the strumming of mandolins and banjos, the tinkle of a piano and youthful voices singing "O, Promise me," or "Only a Bird in a Gilded Cage."

To the west, as the train moved north from 110th Street, was Morningside Heights, the site of New York's new "civic acropolis": Columbia University (formerly located at Forty-ninth Street and Madison Avenue) with its appropriate "municipal classic" architecture; St. John the Divine Cathedral, European Romanesque in its initial stages but soon to be Gothic in style and the largest religious structure in the country (although, today, still unfinished); and St. Luke's Hospital—caretakers of the mind, the soul, and the body. From Morningside Heights, the island descended into the depression of Manhattan Valley and then climbed once more to the rugged topography of Washington Heights, the location of the American League New York Highlanders' Hilltop Park.

As the Sixth Avenue El train passed 120th Street on its way through Harlem, a seventy-foot elevation of rock called "Snake Hill" was visible to the east. This eminence, unsuitable for building, became the center of Mount Morris Park (now Marcus Garvey Memorial Park), a popular walking and picnic area. So attractive was this spot that fine houses were built around it, some comparable to the mansions of Fifth Avenue. Atop the rocky outcrop in Mount Morris Park was one of Manhattan's iron fire towers, used to alert the neighborhood's volunteer firemen. This particular octagonal fire tower is, presently, the last of its kind in New York City.

The Polo Grounds was located just east of the Sixth Avenue El, between 157th and 159th streets. It was made of wood, as all ballparks were, making it extremely vulnerable to the ravages of fire. In the decade 1882–1892, St. Louis' Sportsman Park burned no less than six times. In 1889, Brooklyn's Washington Park lost its double-decked grandstand to fire. The next year, lightning struck the grandstand on Cleveland's Payne Avenue Grounds, splintering and charring it badly. There were four major ballpark fires in 1894. Baltimore's Union Park was nearly destroyed. Boston's elaborate South End Grounds was completely wiped out, along with hundreds of wooden buildings in the residential neighborhood across the street. Flames roared through Chicago's West Side Grounds in the middle of a game, leaving enormous damage and forty injured spectators. Philadelphia's Huntington Street Grounds suffered the total incineration of its main stands from a blaze touched off by a plumber's stove. And, in 1901, Cincinnati had its grandstand burned down. It was not until 1909, with the opening of Shibe Park in Philadelphia and Forbes Field in Pittsburgh, that the era of concrete and steel came to baseball stadia and the threat of conflagration was considerably reduced.

Admission to a major league ball game ranged from $.25 to $1.00, depending upon where you sat, with the individual seats beneath the covered grandstand being the most expensive and the boards of the exposed "bleachers" being the cheapest. This at a time when the average American earned $.22 an hour, while a dozen eggs cost $.12, a shave $.15, a hat $2.00 and one of those newfangled automobiles $1,550. But the admission price was not the total out-of-pocket amount likely to be spent. Once inside the park, there were all sorts of good things to purchase. Seated on a rented cushion, a hungry and thirsty krank could stop any of the numerous vendors selling peanuts, hot dogs, sandwiches, wedges of pie, soft drinks, and beer. A day at the ballpark could not be a very casual financial event for a working-class New Yorker. In fact, it was the middle class that provided the great bulk of the population baseball organizations aimed to attract. Since the New York State "blue law" forbade professional entertainment on Sundays as a desecration of the Sabbath, and a working-class job involved every day but Sunday, the middle class had to be the target audience.

Waiting for the Giant players and fans in 1904, on the site of the old ticket office on Eighth Avenue, was a totally new clubhouse which *The New York Times* thought was "the handsomest and most complete building on any baseball ground in the country." The third and highest floor was made into a huge gymnasium. Below it were the locker and lounging rooms, and baths and showers. And the ground floor housed business offices and served as a twelve-gate distribution center that funneled spectators to every section, including the newly enlarged outfield stands. The facilities on the top two floors, however, were, as was the custom of the day, for the home team only. The visiting team put on their uniforms at their hotel and took a horse-drawn open carriage to the field. Owners believed this provided a good source of advertisement for the game. Jimmy Austin, third baseman with the Highlanders and St. Louis Browns, remembers this ride as "a lot of fun. Kids running alongside as we went past, and rotten tomatoes once in a while. Always lots of excitement when the ball club rode by, you know, with plenty of yelling back and forth, as you can imagine." One can also imagine that it was *not* a lot of fun when those tomatoes or more substantial missiles found their targets after a tough, nerve-wracking game.

Down the lines in the Polo Grounds, all uncovered seats were rebuilt and set in concrete foundations, rather than the old wooden mudsills. And the upper grandstand was renovated so that each of its boxes could accommodate six people. Furthermore, the Giants' playing field, which was in the hands of the imaginative Tom Murphy, the old Oriole groundskeeper, was raised three to four feet to provide a more reliable surface. But this was not all the congenial, mustachioed Tom could do with the home grounds. Back in Baltimore his special contouring and doctoring was the stuff of legends. He could take the third base line and shape it so that bunts had to remain fair; he could mix, wet, and roll the infield to make sure that "Baltimore chops" would bounce out of reach for base hits; and he could hide finely shaved soap around the mound so that enemy pitchers who tried to dry their perspiring hands on the dirt would see their best deliveries sail off in various unplanned directions. The condition of the field was a perpetual source of difficulty for the best of players. "Now the lowest minor leagues have better fields to play on than we had in the major leagues," asserted Pittsburg third baseman-outfielder Tommy Leach. "You never knew how a ball was going to bounce in those days. Lots of times we'd get a rake and go out and rake the grounds around our own position." Bennett Park, in Detroit, presented a singular challenge. The field was located on the site of an old hay market, originally paved with cobblestones. When the few inches of loam that spread over these cobblestones was displaced, balls would suddenly take the weirdest of bounces. An error in this park would just bring a shrug of the shoulders and the comment, "It hit another cobble." Indeed, a photograph of the Polo Grounds shows that a cobble was not necessary to make a bouncing ball erratic; those numerous bare and scrub spots that can clearly be seen from the center field view would be enough to do the trick. And, if the irregular playing surface didn't cause problems, the bats and catcher's gear dropped in front of the players' benches and near home plate, the mitts left on the field by the team at bat, and the umpire's broom—long-handled in the American League—occasionally did.

The typical New York fan who walked through the new twelve-gate entrance to the Polo Grounds was dressed in proper public attire—that is, a dark jacket, tie, and derby or straw hat. Accompanied women were encouraged to come to the ballpark and expected to locate themselves in sheltered grandstand seats. In fact, they were accorded free admission on Ladies Day because their presence, it was believed, had a civilizing effect on the often unruly crowd. However, for the most part, the stands were filled with uniformly clad males, ranging from several thousand on a weekday to 10,000 on a Saturday, with as many as 20,000 or more for special games and holidays. Irishmen and Germans were the most rabid baseball fans. These groups, having been in the United

States in large numbers since the mid-nineteenth century, had already established themselves to some large extent and taken an "American" orientation. Regarding the more recent immigrants from southern and eastern Europe, baseball was simply not part of their desperate world.

As an acknowledgement of the great number of stalwart Irish rooters in the center field bleachers in the Polo Grounds, this section was commonly referred to as "Burkeville." Some of the regulars out there even became celebrities. Frank B. "Well, Well" Wood, an electrical engineer with the stocky build, large mustache, and derby that made him representative of the boys, would add to the drama by bellowing the phrase that earned him his nickname and led to a Zane Grey short story. Runners were streaking around the bases, wrote Grey:

> I gripped my seat strangling the uproar within me. Where was the applause? The fans were silent, choked as I was, but from a different cause. Cless crossed the plate with the score that defeated New York; still the tension never laxed until Burt beat the ball home in as beautiful a run as ever thrilled an audience.
>
> In the bleak dead pause of amazed disappointment Old Well-Well lifted his hulking figure and loomed, towered over the bleachers. His wide shoulders spread, his broad chest expanded, his transfigured face shone with a glorious light. Then, as he threw back his head and opened his lips, his face turned purple, the muscles of his cheeks and jaw rippled and strung, the veins on his forehead swelled into bulging ridges. Even the back of his neck grew red.
>
> "Well! Well! Well!"
>
> Ear-splitting stentorian blast! For a moment I was deafened. But I heard the echo ringing from the cliff, a pealing clarion call, beautiful and wonderful, winding away in hollow reverberation, then breaking out

anew from building to building in clear con-
catenation.

Few blacks could be seen in the crowds attending a major
league game because major league baseball was an exclusively white affair and had been so for two decades. But
blacks in professional baseball went back at least as far as
John "Bud" Fowler, who received money for playing on a
white team in New Castle, Pennsylvania, in 1872. In 1884,
Moses Fleetwood Walker became the first black major leag-
uer, catching for Toledo of the American Association.
Through the next few years, a small but increasing number of
blacks entered the minor leagues, and then, in 1887, the
trouble began. That year the International League established the first color ban, and "Cap" Anson, of the Chicago
White Stockings, the most talented, successful, and influential player and manager in the National League, made an
ugly issue of competing against a team with a black man on
it—Newark's George Stovey. Anson's attitude and action was
the sharpest noise in the swelling cacophony of racist objec-
tions that cleared blacks from all leagues by the turn of the
century. "Jim Crow," that post-Reconstruction backlash of
bigotry, had hit baseball with great impact, and skilled black
players were now restricted to the all-black teams that naturally began to proliferate. The "separate but equal" doctrine,
which gained the sanction of the Supreme Court in *Plessy* v.
Ferguson (1896), quickly and destructively wormed its way
into the "national pastime" and deprived many excellent
ballplayers of the opportunity to use their proficiencies on
the highest level. What they had to settle for as "separate"
was decidedly unequal. With no black faces on major league
fields, there was little reason to expect there would be black
faces in the stands either.

So, the New York fan who would travel far uptown to the
Polo Grounds to see a ball game was, for the most part, a

white middle-class male of Irish or German background. What the American League had to consider was whether this fan would travel a little further uptown to 165th Street and Fort Washington Avenue, ten blocks north and half a mile west of the last stop on the Sixth Avenue El, and put up with a bit rougher accommodations, to see a new team struggle for respectability in a new league. The Giants had their diehards, who provided 20 percent of the attendance at National League games. Was Manhattan Island big enough for two favorite teams?

The political struggle during the "Great Baseball War" to find a piece of real estate that would serve as a playing field for the nascent New York American League franchise was fierce enough to result in the slimmest of pickings for Frank Farrell and Bill Devery. The property that they finally rented, on the basis of a ten-year lease, would cost $10,000 annually. It was owned by the New York Institute for the Blind and was located, according to *Sporting Life*, on

> a plot of hilly ground, dotted by large and small boulders and trees, many of them dead, with a pond extending along the roadway side that will have to be filled in. Masses of rock are grouped where the grandstand is to be erected. There is not a level spot ten feet square on the whole property. From Broadway, looking west, the ground starts in a low swamp filled with water, and runs up into a ridge of rocks perhaps twelve or fifteen feet above the level of Broadway. The rocks will be blasted out and the swamp filled in, while 100 trees will have to be pulled up.

The contract for remodeling this unlikely terrain went to Thomas McAvoy, one of the club's minority stockholders and the Tammany leader of the Twenty-third Assembly District, not coincidentally the area in which the new park was to be built. McAvoy had a gigantic task before him. Ban Johnson later stated that "we had to use so much dynamite that if unleashed at exactly the same second it would have blown up half of New York." At its highest point, the rock that had to be removed reached fifty feet above ground level. But McAvoy would be paid handsomely for the labor he hired and the wooden park he assembled—that's the way things were done in this city.

The next task was to get New Yorkers to warm up to their Washington Heights team. This fell to president Joseph Gordon, operator of a prosperous coal and wood business and former Deputy Superintendent of Buildings. In truth, Gordon was a figurehead whose main function was to give the American League's New York entry a cleaner face than the ones presented by Frank Farrell and Bill Devery. However, he could be trusted with thinking of a nickname for the team, and the process seems to have begun during a conversation that the president had with members of the New York press. One reporter suggested the "Islanders," "because they had landed on [Manhattan] island." Another thought that since the club would do well, the name should indicate something elevated. To this Gordon replied, "Then we'll call them the Highlanders." The choice seemed appropriate for additional reasons: the ballpark site just hacked out of Manhattan's Upper West Side rested on one of the highest spots in the borough, and the appellation was already familiar because of the "Gordon Highlanders," a crack Scottish regiment known to many in the English-speaking world. This last connection pleased the president and those who could accept the martial glories of Britannia, but New York's Irish population objected to this reminder of the terrible subjugation of their homeland. As a protest, they, from the outset, called this team the "Yankees," a name that, by 1913, came to replace "Highlanders" altogether. "Yankees" also had the advantage of being easier to fit into a one-column headline, and, so, it received the approval of the New York press.

In their first year of operation, 1903, the Highlanders did modestly well on the field, finishing fourth in the eight-team American League (the National had the same number of clubs), and at the gate, averaging a reasonable 2,000–3,000 fans per home game. Preparing for the 1904 season, Farrell and Devery made some improvements in American League Park—more often called Hilltop park, or just "the Hilltop." The large gully in right field was filled in and the fence was moved back 20 feet so that it was now 420 feet from home plate. With the left field fence at 365 feet and the center field fence at 542 feet, there was ample room for the Highlander outfielders to catch fly balls. This was a typical arrangement in the early days of the twentieth century and had to do with the fact that fans expected and enjoyed footrace extra-base hits and appreciated the unlikely event of the "dead ball" being knocked out of a park of any legitimate size. Before the introduction of cork centers in 1911 and the modern lively ball in 1920, the game revolved around a wound yarn sphere wrapped in horsehide that was left in play regardless of its condition. "As a Philadelphia boy," recalled Fred Lieb, "I saw a game at the Philly National Park about this time in which the umpire proudly finished the game with the same ball with which he started." Cincinnati Reds outfielder Eddie Roush remembered catching "many a ball in the outfield that was mashed on one side. Come bouncing out there like a jumping bean." Since the long ball was not going to be hit very often, the kranks just did not figure it in their expected fun for the afternoon. Furthermore, a great deal of space in front of the fence made ideal standing room for "overflow crowds"—that is, crowds that outnumbered the seats. Building additional bench areas cost money; stretching a rope behind the outfield accommodated paying customers at no expense at all. The further the fence, the more the standing room and the more the income—baseball was a business, after all.

Also altered at the Hilltop for the 1904 season was the scoreboard down the left field foul line. It was enlarged so that the figures could now be seen in the grandstand behind home plate. This effort to provide the hometown rooters with better information ran counter to the general practice. Usually, owners deliberately limited communication with the public so that the scorecards would sell better. The pitcher and catcher, together called the "battery" because they, like a team attending a cannon, were responsible for launching the ball, might be announced by megaphone just before game time, but the rest of the line-ups and line-up changes often were not. Even the scorecard was of little assistance because it had several names written at one position, and players did not wear numbers on their backs until the 1930s. But the Highlanders were fighting to draw fans into the ballpark and had to make their place more presentable. Everything counted in the fight to cut into the Giants' long-standing Manhattan market.

On no other day did the home club plan so much to win the favor of the local folk as the first game of the season. The opening ceremonies and contest could be expected to draw well over 10,000 people despite the cold April weather in the East and the Midwest, the geographical extent of major league baseball at the time. Early in the year, reports circulated that both Manhattan clubs demanded home dates for their first game. *The New York Times* commented that if these reports were true, "the thin veneer of peace which has existed for over a year between the major baseball leagues may be broken by an upheaval of the turbulent wave of trouble which has been gathering for many months." However, when the league schedules were formally exchanged, the nature of the conflict had been altered a bit. The Highlanders still planned to open at home, but the Giants scheduled their first game on the road in Brooklyn. The problem with this, according to Ban Johnson, was that he had been assured that the Giants would not play in the metropolitan area at all on this day. To substantiate his claim that Pittsburg owner Barney Dreyfuss and Brooklyn Superba owner Charley Ebbets had broken faith, Johnson stated that he would produce the minutes of the joint conference meeting during which Dreyfuss had announced that Boston would open in Brooklyn and the Giants would open in Philadelphia. Johnson argued:

> It was distinctly understood that no changes were to be made after the schedules were completed, and we did not alter ours. The National League changed several dates, and the one affecting the Brooklyn opening is especially distasteful. . . . The American League is not to be trifled with.

When he got back to Chicago, where the main American League office was located, he intended to take the matter up with Jim Hart, owner of the National League Chicago Colts (already called the Cubs by many) and chairman of the Joint Schedule Committee:

> Failing to come to any satisfactory understanding with him, I propose taking it up with Mr. [Garry] Herrmann, as Chairman of the National Commission [which governed organized baseball]. In the event that Mr. Herrmann and I cannot agree I will consider myself absolved from any further obligations to the National League. Then the American League playing dates will be readjusted to suit the best interests of the organization.

National League President Harry Pulliam dismissed Johnson's threat to take the schedule affair up with Herrmann as having no relevance to the National League decision-making process and indignantly denied any wrongdoing. Ebbets, Brush, and Dreyfuss also issued denials of trickery, with the last named threatening to "make an affi-davit to that effect . . . and have it published in every paper in the country, even if [he had] to pay for the insertions [himself]."

It was Ban Johnson's single-minded determination to pro-tect and nurture the American League that hardened his stand on the issue of opening day in Greater New York. The Highlanders had to make it in the greatest of cities if the circuit was truly to be regarded as a major league. Johnson well knew that Giant fans were very loyal and would think nothing of crossing Brooklyn Bridge in the April chill to see their team perform. In fact, the National League was ada-mant in its decision to have the Giants play their first game in the borough of churches and trolleys. Pulliam told the press that the matter would receive no further discussion: the schedule was set as it had been published. That such was the unalterable case was made evident by the softened American League words uttered from Manhattan. Frank Farrell calmly explained that he wanted no rupture between the leagues over the schedule disagreement. His team would proceed with its plans to begin the 1904 campaign hosting Boston.

The major leagues were about to enter their second year of peaceful coexistence. But few, at this time, could doubt that the hard feelings would erupt in some way through the long, hot summer and the tension-ridden fall. New York was the best bet for the site of that eruption because there the management of the Giants, the organization that once had the city to itself, was still unreconciled to the idea of company on the island of Manhattan, especially when that company was the favored child of Ban Johnson.

4.

Assembling New York's Teams

A t the very end of the 1902 season, John McGraw, on the job in New York since July, had a Giant club that finished last, 53½ games out, with a 48–88 record. A year later, he had a Giant club that finished second, 6½ games out, with an 84–55 record.

The largest but not the only part of McGraw's leadership role consisted of changing those whom he was leading. As soon as he arrived on the scene, he took hold of the Giants' roster and crossed off nine names. "You can begin by releasing these," he told a startled Andrew Freedman. Freedman replied that the players he had just discarded cost him $14,000. "If you keep them," warned McGraw, "they'll cost you more. I've brought real ballplayers with me and I'll get some more." Joining the Giants at this point were former Oriole pitchers Joe McGinnity and Jack Cronin, first baseman Dennis "Dan" McGann, and utility man "Duke" Roger Bresnahan. And, right after the season ended, former Oriole shortstop Bill Gilbert also became a Giant. There had not been much to see at the Polo Grounds in quite a while. The last league championships, in fact the only ones, were won in 1888 and 1889 when the team earned the nickname that stuck with it ever after. But now the stands began to fill up. McGraw's new players were promising, and the volatile manager was a show all by himself. New Yorkers "began to pile into the park almost as much in anticipation of some new show of wild anger as to see two teams play baseball," remarks baseball historian Robert Smith.

The 1903 Giants had McGann at first; Gilbert was switched to second; rookie Charley Babb did a creditable job at short; and Bill Lauder had an improved year at third. The catchers were Jack Warner and "Niagara" Frank Bowerman, two unpleasant characters who, nevertheless, made the plays behind the plate and helped with the attack. Warner was a bigoted anti-Hibernian in an age when so many players and fans were of Irish background; and Bowerman was a surly man who was not above, as Blanche McGraw reported, racing a lady for a stool on a Brooklyn-New York ferryboat and having her arrested after the subsequent verbal altercation led to his face being slapped. The Giant outfield was really fine. The right fielder was the fleet-footed George Browne, obtained from the Phillies the previous year for cash. Browne, in his third campaign, hit .313 and stole 27 bases. In left field was "Sandow" Sam Mertes, a veteran who hit .280, drove in a league-leading 104 runs, and stole 45 bases. And the center fielder was Roger Bresnahan, a real star in the making. Bresnahan was, in many ways, a hard man to pin down. While he claimed to have been born in Ireland—and, for that reason, came to be known as the "Duke of Tralee"—he actually came from and lived his whole life in Toledo, Ohio. And then, for the first four years of his career, he pitched, caught, and played first, short, third, and the outfield. However, in 1903, McGraw stationed him in center field and at the top of the batting order. The "Duke" responded by hitting .350 (.005 off the average that earned Honus Wagner the batting title) and stealing 34 bases. The real story in the improvement of the Giants, however, was the superb pitching of right-handers Joe McGinnity and young Christy Mathewson.

Hitting against Joe McGinnity was a frustrating affair. While he was second in the league in strikeouts in 1903, he did not often try to make the hitter miss altogether. "He was the sort who made batters smile confidently as they stepped to the plate," explains Smith,

> and kick the dirt around afterward while they complained the guy had nothing on the ball. Oh, they could hit Joe's pitch all right. But try to meet that swift-rising, looping pitch with anything more than the edge of the bat! Bloop! would go the ball into the air as the batter caught the under side of it. Or down it would spin into the dirt as the batter, misjudging the drop, would viciously top it. The damn pitch never came straight at you. It started near Joe's shoes, for his fingers almost scraped the ground as he completed the pitch. And it appeared to be approaching crossways and upward, looking big enough to be broken in two, but always just escaping the full weight of the bat.

"Old Sal" is what McGinnity called his underhand curve— and you had better be ready for "Old Sal" as soon as you stepped into the box. As teammate Fred Snodgrass recalled, "If you were looking at your feet or something, the way they do today to get just the right position and all, well, by that time the ball would already be in the catcher's mitt. . . . The catcher would throw [him] the ball and bang, right back it would come!" All McGinnity did, in addition to striking out 171 hitters that year, was lead the National League in wins, 31 (losing 20); in complete games, 46 or 44 depending on the source (if 46, it was the most in modern National League

history); and in innings pitched, 434, which is the un-
disputed modern National League record. And finally—contributing to his "Iron Man" identification (the name was
actually gained from working in his father-in-law's iron fac-
tory)—McGinnity, during the month of August, pitched and
won three complete double-headers. In these six games, he
allowed an average of 6 hits and less than 2 runs. McGinnity
was not an impressive physical speciman. He was 5 feet 11, a
chubby 206 pounds, with a small round face and almost
comical eyebrows. But he had that excellent control, which
makes for economy of pitches, and that easy submarine
delivery that literally enabled him to pitch all day long.

Giant pitcher Christy Mathewson was born into a financially comfortable Factoryville, Pennsylvania, farming family
of British origin. His background appeared to be manifested
in his assured bearing: he always seemed to exhibit, as Fred
Lieb put it, "the reserve and reticence of the British gentry."
His size, 6 feet 1½ inches and 195 pounds, and strength,
together with a roundhouse curve, allowed him great success
on the amateur level. However, he also managed to pick up a
reverse curve, a screwball or "fadeaway," which he would
later develop fully. Formal education was a family expecta-
tion, so Christy traveled to nearby Lewisburg and enrolled at
Bucknell. There drop-kicking a football as well as pitching a
baseball took up his extracurricular time. One morning, in
the winter of 1900, Christy was approached by a man who
called himself "Phenomenal" Ed Smith. Smith planned to
operate a Norfolk franchise in the Virginia League and
wanted Mathewson to sign a contract for $80 a month and
pitch for him. Christy, whose Bucknell team had a game
against the University of Pennsylvania that afternoon, went
out and kicked field goals of 42 and 45 yards to help upset the
favored Ivy school. Smith raised the salary offer to $90 a
month and Christy eventually signed. By July, he had started
22 games and won 20 of them.

The next stop for Mathewson was the major leagues. The Phillies, Athletics, and Reds wanted him, but he ended up in New York with the Giants. Norfolk was to be given $1,500 on the conditional basis that Mathewson make the big jump to the National League successfully. However, the twenty-year-old right-hander had trouble finding the plate. After six appearances, he had a 0–3 record and an ERA of 4.76. So it was back to Norfolk, and the Giants recovered their $1,500. When the season ended, John T. Brush, then owner of the Cincinnati Reds, drafted Mathewson for $100 and immediately dealt him back to the Giants for Amos Rusie, a famed fireballer who had not played in two years. Six or seven years before, when the "Hoosier Thunderbolt" was the best in the business, this would have been a very sharp swap on Brush's part. From 1890 to 1895, Rusie led the National League in strikeouts five times, finishing second the year he was not the champ. During those same years, he averaged 30 wins and 483 innings pitched. It was said he threw so hard that he was principally responsible for the decision, in 1893, to move the pitching distance back from the official fifty feet (actually fifty-five feet because of a pitcher's box arrangement that required back line contact) to sixty feet six inches. "He was to baseball then," claims Burt Hawkins, "what Babe Ruth was to baseball later." But Rusie had taken the years 1896 and 1899 off in bitter salary disputes with Andrew Freedman, and, in 1900, marital problems monopolized all his time and concentration, and he never pitched beyond spring training. In 1901, when he was ready to resume his career, he found that he had been traded to Cincinnati for the unproven Christy Mathewson. Rusie had to show he could still pitch in the big leagues, but Mathewson had to show he could pitch there in the first place. Going into the 1901 season, the jury had to be out on this swap. After the campaign, the verdict was that Brush had made the worst deal of his administrative life. So great an advantage did New York gain in this trade that, years later, Brush was charged with planning to buy the Giants and, for that reason, cleverly sending the great Mathewson ahead to wait for him. Certainly Christy was very good that first full year with the Giants. He won 20 (lost 17), completed 36 games, struck out 221, and walked only 97—evidence of his increased mastery of the strike zone, a special skill for which he would become famous. Furthermore, on July 15, he threw a no-hitter (the first of two he would have in his career) against the St. Louis Cardinals. Rusie, on the other hand, produced worse than nothing. Appearing in three games, his record was 0–1, with an ERA of 8.59. The Mathewson-for-Rusie trade now looked very peculiar. In Norfolk, club officials screamed loudly that they had been cheated out of $1,400 in a dirty deal cooked up between those robber barons Brush and Freedman.

Mathewson had a rougher year in 1902, winning 14 and losing 17 for the last-place Giants. However, he did have 8 shutouts, a 2.11 ERA, and 162 strikeouts—all of which indicated that his record would have been better with a better club. In late July, with the arrival of John McGraw, the chances of a better club in the near future were very real. The young twenty-nine-year-old manager immediately made the young twenty-two-year-old pitcher his major project. Mathewson was married early in 1903, and when the Giants returned from spring training, Christy and his wife Jane joined the McGraws in renting a ground-floor apartment on Columbus Avenue and Eighty-fifth Street, right near the Sixth Avenue El. "We had seven rooms, which cost $50 a month," Blanche McGraw recalled. "John paid the rent and gas bill and Christy paid for the food which totalled about the same, since the men traveled half the summer." Such shared apartments were not unusual at the turn of the century when New York City was filling up with immigrants and fortune-seeking Americans, and housing, especially of the decent kind, was in short supply. The friendship between McGraw and Mathewson became a firm one and lasted their lifetimes. Christy was the only player permitted to call McGraw by his first name—he was "Mr. McGraw" to everyone else.

What McGraw most appreciated about the diamond of a pitcher emerging from the rough was his ability to think, learn, and improve. "I never had to tell Christy anything a second time," said the manager noted for his stinginess with a compliment. "Within a few years he had charted nearly every ballplayer in the National League. . . . He also began working on his control. By watching McGinnity, he picked up the idea of the change of pace and perfected it." With his two years of well-processed experience and refined approach and tools, "Matty," as he came to be known, was prepared to make 1903 a big year—and it certainly turned out that way. He started 42 games, completing 37 (second in the league to McGinnity); won 30 while losing 13; and struck out a league-leading 267 hitters. "Matty" had become a confident as well as talented pitcher. He had acquired the conviction that every hitter he faced was a decided inferior.

For McGraw to make a move upward from second place in 1904, the infield would have to be improved. And this is what the determined manager with the free hand set about doing. His shortstop in 1903 was Charley Babb, one of those rare ballplayers from far-away Oregon. Babb was a rookie, but considering his lack of experience, he had a good year: .248 batting average in 121 games and a solid defensive performance at a premier position. However, McGraw was looking for a pennant, and he had his eye on someone better—a veteran. For the last five years, Bill Dahlen, known as "Bad Bill" or "Bull Head," had covered shortstop for Brooklyn in the reliable manner that comes from some real talent enhanced by a lot of daily work. Dahlen had previously played the same position for the Chicago Colts right through the 1890s. He was no shrinking violet, this "Bad

Bill." Fred Lieb remembered him as "a vexation to all his managers." He liked to throw the ball in the dirt just to make Chicago manager "Cap" Anson squirm. However, Dahlen's insistence on asserting himself paid off for Chicago and then Brooklyn in that he was one of the first shortstops to demand to know what pitch was being thrown and, as a result of his insight, to position the other fielders by relaying this information. This was "inside baseball" and McGraw loved it. In December, a deal with Brooklyn was negotiated. McGraw could have Dahlen if he parted with Babb and pitcher Jack Cronin, who just concluded his sixth year in the majors. Cronin was a 6-foot-tall right-hander whom McGraw thought enough of to bring along when he jumped from the American League. But Cronin had not pitched very much (6–4 record in 20 appearances) on a staff so totally dominated by McGinnity and Mathewson. McGraw seized the offer:

> Now I have the man I have wanted ever since I have had charge of this team. There is no better shortstop in baseball than Dahlen. To some, he may appear lazy and indifferent, but I notice that when the gong sounds to begin the game he pricks up his ears like a war horse and never misses a trick.
>
> The Giants will play to some very large crowds next season, abroad as well as at home. Dahlen is an iceberg before a big assemblage of rooters and does not know what it is to get rattled. He is the kind of man every club needs to steady the infield.

Still, there was one more infield position McGraw wanted improved. Bill Lauder began his career with the Phillies in 1898, but by 1902, he returned to his native Manhattan as the regular Giant third baseman. He hit .288 in 1902 and .314 in 1903. Nevertheless, McGraw thought he could do better with a kid named Art Devlin, whom he saw play in Newark. Devlin was a graduate of Georgetown University and gave the appearance of being the smart and fearless hot-corner guardian the Giant manager believed he needed to work the left side with Dahlen. Perhaps they could no longer get away with the overt intimidation that was the trademark of the old Orioles, but Dahlen and Devlin would not allow a base runner an easy time scoring from second.

Others on the Giant roster going into the 1904 season were utility man Jack Dunn, outfielder Harry "Moose" Mc-Cormick, and pitchers Luther "Dummy" Taylor, Leon "Red" Ames, and George "Hooks" Wiltse. Dunn had been around since 1897, when he pitched and played the outfield and infield for Brooklyn. Since then, he had performed his versatile services for the Phillies, McGraw's American League Orioles, and, for the past two years, the Giants. Not a great anything, Dunn was a good enough everything to fill in if a regular were injured for a brief while. In 1903, he hit .241, playing 27 games at short, 25 at third, 19 at second, and 1 in the outfield. "Dunnie" fit McGraw's description of a winning temperament. He was, according to Fred Lieb, "easily riled and ready to fight at the drop of a hat." Later, when he became a tremendously successful owner-manager of the International League Baltimore Orioles, he had the great distinction of signing and helping to refine the talents of a young left-handed pitcher out of St. Mary's Industrial School named George Ruth. Since George was a minor, Dunn had to sign a court order making him responsible for monitoring the boy's often errant behavior. Some said that George got his nickname because of this relationship—he was Dunn's "Babe."

Luther Taylor was one of two deaf mutes to play in the major leagues, the other one being Bill Hoy, an outfielder who played from 1888 through 1902. Hoy is credited by some with being responsible for hand signs given by umpires on balls and strikes. Both Taylor and Hoy, in unfortunate accordance with the high level of insensitivity of the times, were known as "Dummy." Taylor began his career with the Giants in 1900 and returned to them in 1902 after a brief fling in the American League with the Cleveland Blues. In 1903, he had a 13–13 record in 33 appearances. He was the third pitcher on the Giant staff and was likely to play a significant role in shouldering the mound responsibilities in 1904. To this point, his major impact on the club was pressuring the Giant players into learning sign language. "We could all read and speak the deaf-and-dumb sign language," attested Fred Snodgrass,

> because Dummy Taylor took it as an affront if you didn't learn to converse with him. He wanted to be one of us, to be a full-fledged member of the team. If we went to the vaudeville show, he wanted to know what the joke was, and somebody had to tell him. So we all learned. We practiced all the time. We'd go by elevated train from the hotel to the Polo Grounds, and all during the ride we'd be spelling out the advertising signs. Not talking to one another, but sitting there spelling out the advertising messages. Even today, when I pass a billboard I find myself doing it.

McGraw was supposed to have taken advantage of this special team communication skill by sitting on the bench, out in the open, spelling out such signals as S–T–E–A–L, "so plain," said Snodgrass, "that anyone in the park who could read deaf-and-dumb language would know what was happening."

"Red" Ames, a right-hander, did not have much of an opportunity to pitch with the Giants in 1903, but he was extremely effective when he was in there. He completed and won the two games he started, pitched a shutout in one of them, had an ERA of 1.29, and struck out 14. "Hooks" Wiltse, the only lefty on the pitching staff, was a rookie. He had a reputation as an exceptional fielder and a decent hitter. Every contribution mattered for a newcomer who hoped to stick on a roster of fifteen players.

The manager of the New York Highlanders, the man who got the job McGraw once wanted so badly that his disappointment prompted his jump to the Giants, was Clark Griffith. Griffith had been one of the earliest migrants to the American League, serving as raider, manager, and pitcher for the Chicago White Sox. It was Griffith who, after attending the Players Protective Association's sour meeting with National League owners, gave the signal to Ban Johnson: "Go ahead; you can get all the players you want. . . ." And it was Griffith who won the American League's first pennant, in 1901, contributing 24 wins (against 7 losses) himself, which amounted to a league-leading .774 percentage. Although the White Sox dropped to fourth in 1902 and his own record slipped to 15–9, Griffith remained a very capable leader and performer in the eyes of Ban Johnson. He was not always the "good guy," however. In fact, he had the reputation of being one of the worst complainers on the field in either league. Fred Lieb called him "an apt pupil of Cry Baby Anson, cantankerous and ever ready to whine at any umpire who failed to give him the last one-sixty-fourth of an inch." But, Lieb continued, "off the field he was a man of charm, great ability and character, one destined to go high in his profession." After the 1902 season ended, Johnson chose Griffith to move to New York to organize the team recently purchased by Frank Farrell and Bill Devery.

The first players on the New York American League club's roster were Oriole holdovers, the only valuable ones being veterans Jimmy "Buttons" Williams, a second baseman, and "Handsome Harry" Howell, a right-handed pitcher. From the 1902 pennant-winning Philadelphia Athletics came Dave Fultz, an outfielder who hit .300 in his three full years in the majors and the past year's league leader in runs scored. All the rest came from the minors or the National League. Of very special note among the latter were "Wee Willie" Keeler, who crossed the East River from his native Brooklyn, and the half-dozen players who left the National League champion Pittsburg Pirates.

Outfielder Willie Keeler was one of the most amazing and best-loved players in the game's history. He began his major league career with the Giants, but it was as a Baltimore Oriole and a Brooklyn Superba that he became a star. The little man—5 feet 4, 140 pounds, at best (he wouldn't allow himself to be measured or weighed)—had the respect of the toughest and most experienced players and writers. Johnny "the Crab" Evers, the shrewd and pugnacious second baseman, thought he "was perhaps the greatest judge of where batters would hit that ever played, and in addition his quickness of perception gave him a running start after every fly ball." Fences did not frighten "Wee Willie" any. Jim Price recounted a catch he made in Washington, when a drive to right seemed about to clear the rusty barrier behind him. Willie leaped, put his left arm through the wire, and caught the ball barehanded. "It was the greatest catch I ever saw in my long career as a baseball writer and sports editor," Price asserted.

However, it was not as a fielder that Willie Keeler made his most indelible mark in the minds of contemporaries and the columns of the all-time record book. This came as the wielder of a tiny thirty-inch twenty-nine ounce magical wooden wand. He was quiet and unassuming—"a Lilliputian on a swarming field of snarling giants," according to baseball historian Lee Allen. Keeler "walked to the plate as if to apologize for intruding, stepping as softly as a cat. He never rubbed his hands in the dirt, never pulled down his cap or clutched at his belt." It was in the box on the left side that he assumed his slightly crouched stance, his bat choked and held with a spread-handed grip, and his intense dark eyes locked on the pitcher's arm. His objective, he once told Abe Yager of the *Brooklyn Daily Eagle*, was simple: "Hit 'em where they ain't." And this he surely did very often. From 1894, his first season in Baltimore, through 1902, his last season in Brooklyn, he annually hit around .375, with over 200 hits, 135 runs scored, and 40 stolen bases. Even with these impressive statistics, Keeler's accomplishments in 1897 stood out as spectacular. This was the year he began with a 44-game hitting streak and ended with a .432 batting average, supported by 243 hits and decorated by 64 stolen bases. Only Joe DiMaggio hit in more consecutive games (56), although Pete Rose hit in as many, and only Hugh Duffy hit for a higher average (.438). "Beyond any question," said pitching great Charley "Kid" Nichols, "Keeler was the smartest hitter I ever faced. He could do everything with the bat." Not only was he able to drop bunts down both lines, slap grounders into all the holes, and send little flares to any part of the outfield, but if he got his pitch, he could tag one, too. Nichols remembered a game in Baltimore

> when Big Dan Brouthers of the Orioles, a powerful slugger, hit a home run over the center field fence for the first time. They put a flag on top of the fence to mark the spot where the ball disappeared from view. But, the next week, little Willie duplicated Big Dan's homer, and the flag was taken down.

What it took to attract the great Keeler was $10,000, the largest amount of money paid to any player during the "Great Baseball War." What Johnson got was guaranteed excitement for New York American League fans and added credibility for his ascending enterprise.

The Pittsburg Pirates had won the National League pennant from 1901 through 1903. A fundamental reason for their success was the decision by Ban Johnson not to raid Barney Dreyfuss's club. The plan, according to Eugene Murdock, "was to create such an imbalance of talent in the National that the pennant race would be uninteresting and attendance would decline." Moreover, Johnson apparently had some hope that Dreyfuss might be persuaded to shift his whole organization into the American League. However, by the winter of 1902, Johnson abandoned his hope and stuck his sharp raiding ax into the glittering vein of Pirate ballplayers. Murdock sketched out the dramatic scene of the signing of some of the best performers on the best National League team:

> Johnson and [Charles] Somers met catcher-first base-man Jack O'Connor by stealth one night at Pittsburg's Lincoln Hotel. O'Connor brought the players up by the freight elevator to avoid confrontation with Dreyfuss and Pulliam, who had learned something was afoot and had camped out in the hotel lobby. When the night's work was finished, Jesse Tannehill, Jack Chesbro, Tommy Leach, Lefty Davis, Wid Conroy, and O'Connor himself had signed to play with the American League's New York franchise in 1903.

All these furtively secured former Pirates made it to New York except Tommy Leach, who returned to Pittsburg and stayed there for another decade.

The most important player who signed with the Highlanders in the Lincoln Hotel was Jack Chesbro. Although he was called "Happy Jack," he did not spread much joy around the batter's box. His career was gaining momentum rapidly. The first year, 1899, he struggled, winning 6 and losing 10. In his second year, he improved his record to 14–13. Then, in 1901, he made it big: 21–9, for a league-leading .700 percentage and a league-leading 6 shutouts. However, in 1902, he made it bigger: 28–6, for a league-leading percentage of .824 and a league-leading 8 shutouts (tied with two others). Chesbro's fortunes took such a positive turn, in part, because this 5-foot-9, 180-pound right-hander had a will and tenacity to match his bulldog physical dimensions. But his story was also part of a much larger one—the effort by pitchers to regain the upper hand lost by the added five-foot pitching distance marched off in 1893 (officially ten feet, but this doesn't account for where the pitcher had to be standing in the pitcher's box to deliver the ball legally). The first year of the change, the entire league hit .280, 18 points higher than the best team average the previous season. And, in 1894, the league average climbed another 29 points. Obviously, pitchers had to find some way to regain an edge. What they began to do was take advantage of the fact that the ball they threw was changed only when absolutely necessary. Owners were not interested in paying for new baseballs, so the one on the field was kept in play and any that left were retrieved. The result was that under the best of circumstances, the ball was apt to be softened and badly stained. But, what if this semi-natural pitching aid were magnified? What if the ball were deliberately marred so that the pitcher could get a maximum grip and the hitter could not see enough white to hit the delivery squarely? And what if new kinds of deliveries were discovered that would make the marred ball do tricks as it approached the plate? Then the advantage would shift in favor of the pitcher. This is exactly what came to pass in the early years of this century. Sandpaper was used to scuff the surface and produce the "emory ball." Talcum powder or paraffin was used to make a slick spot and produce a "shine ball." And saliva, easily collected from the various substances ballplayers chewed, was used to produce the "spit–ball." It was the spitball that Chesbro learned to control, and this addition to his repertoire suddenly made him an overpowering force. Ty Cobb, whose American League career began in 1905, described what it was like to face "the original master of the spitball": "When Chesbro cranked and fired his overhand spitter—loaded with slippery elm—it came up to the plate like a standard fastball, and then took a diabolical dive under your bat."

Clearly, the Highlanders had a few powerful weapons going into the 1903 season, but Griffith was committed to improving his club in every way and right away. In June, he made a trade with Detroit that helped tremendously. Going to the Tigers were shortstop Herman "Germany" Long, now a mere shadow of the great star he had been years ago with the Boston Beaneaters (later the Braves), and second-year infielder Ernie Courtney. Coming to the Highlanders was shortstop Norman Elberfeld, called "the Tabasco Kid" because of his spicy vocabulary. Elberfeld was in his fifth year and highly regarded as a very tough and able competitor who would find a way to win. "Casey" Stengel, later an Elberfeld protégé, remembered "the Kid" demonstrating the position to take to get hit by a pitch and the mock anger needed to cover the stunt. And Ty Cobb, an admirer of very few, told another Elberfeld anecdote with obvious appreciation. Cobb, in his rookie year, was on first.

> I went sprinting to second and slid head-first at the bag. Kid Elberfeld was waiting to give me the professional "teach"—which he did by slamming his knee down on the back of my neck, grinding my face untenderly into the dirt. Spluttering and spitting dirt, I heard Umpire O'Loughlin's well-rounded baritone—"Owwwtttt!"
>
> I walked, or sort of crept, away from there with some skin scraped off. And with the Kid grinning at me. . . .
>
> During our next . . . series, I banged into Elberfeld feet-first, caught him by surprise and knocked him kicking onto the grass, while I slid in safely. The Kid was known as a tough number. He got up, shot a stream of tobacco juice, and looked me over reflectively.
>
> "Son, that's how it's done—you've got it," he said. "More power to you."

Elberfeld's style was precisely what John McGraw loved to see operating on a ball field—especially if it was aiding his cause. In fact, for a while, McGraw and Brush believed they had obtained the young firebrand. But the contract he signed with the Giants after the 1902 season was cancelled by the interleague peace commissioners in favor of one he had already signed with the Detroit Tigers. Now, months later, Elberfeld was finally coming to New York—but in a Highlander uniform. Brush was livid with rage. He was totally convinced that Ban Johnson was behind the deal that was designed to hurt his organization at the gate. "Johnson planned to bring Elberfeld to New York all the time," he insisted. "Well, if the Kid can't play with the New York Nationals, we won't stand for him playing with the New York Americans." Nevertheless, Elberfeld's fate was in the hands of men who did not flinch at the empty threats of the Giant owner, and he appeared in Griffith's line-up right on schedule.

Even with Keeler, Chesbro, and Elberfeld, the Highlanders, in what had already become a very strong and competitive American League, could finish no better than fourth in 1903. Griffith would have to do additional tinkering if his team was going to move up in the standings in 1904. In December, he traded Jesse Tannehill, a former Pittsburg ace who had been a bit of a disappointment with his 15–15 record, to Boston for "Long Tom" Hughes. Hughes did not have the high marks that Tannehill had accumulated over nearly a decade, but the big right-hander, with three full seasons behind him, had just won 20 games and lost only 7, for a league-leading percentage of .741. In addition, he hit an impressive .280 in his 93 at-bats. The next month, Harry Howell and Jack O'Connor were sent to the St. Louis Browns for Jack Powell, a hefty right-handed pitcher who was 15–19 in 1903 but had been near or over 20 wins for the previous five years. At about the same time, the contracts of "Deacon" Jim McGuire and Jim "Champ" Osteen were bought from the Detroit Tigers and Washington Senators respectively. McGuire, the grizzled but still capable catcher, managed, in his nineteenth campaign, to hit .250 in 72 games. The nickname "Deacon" usually went to players whose habits were more regular than most. In this case, such a lifestyle paid off. He was around so long, writes Robert Smith, "there were kranks grown to manhood who could not recall when the Deacon had not been playing for money." And no one was tougher behind the plate. Smith tells of the time

> McGuire leaped for the ball, just took a small piece of it with his longest finger, and had the finger bent straight back by the force of the throw. The flesh was stripped right off the bone, neat as a filet of flounder. Bald Bob Emslie, umpiring behind the plate, took one look at the finger and fell in a faint. But the Deacon remained erect, had the finger attended to, and was catching again before the end of the week. "We were short of catchers," he explained.

Osteen, a rookie, appeared in only 10 games at shortstop, had 40 at-bats, and hit an even .200. First baseman "Honest John" Anderson, purchased from the St. Louis Browns, came next. One day, too soon, his name would bring an immediate smile to the faces of knowledgeable baseball fans for attempting to steal second with the bases loaded. From then on, any foolish play was called a "John Anderson," but at this point in his nine-year career, he was known only as a tough out (.284 in 1903, .330 two years before) who would hustle his way from opening to closing day. Catcher Herm McFarland was released and his spot taken by rookie John "Red" Kleinow. And, filling the last two spots on the roster were holdovers: pitcher Bill Wolfe, who had a 6-9 rookie record, with a 2.97 ERA, and journeyman first baseman John Ganzel, who had a serviceable year hitting .277 in 129 games.

The strengthened Giant squad seemed ready to seize the National League flag from the Pittsburg Pirates, and the strengthened Highlander squad seemed ready to challenge for the American League flag, although the current possessors of it were the very powerful Boston Pilgrims (later the Red Sox), winners also of the 1903 World Series, the first played between the two modern major leagues. It was definitely within the realm of possibility that the second modern World Series, in 1904, could be contested by the two teams from Manhattan. That's the way Highlander manager Clark Griffith wanted it to turn out:

> Right here I would like to say that no man in Greater New York will pull harder for the Giants to win the National League pennant than I will, for this reason. As I understand it, the two leagues have decided that there shall be a post-season series of five games between the pennant winners in the respective races to decide the world's championship. Should the Highlanders be lucky enough to win our pennant and the Giants have the good fortune to win theirs, we will then come together in a series of games. In that case I am positive that we can convince the baseball public that the Highlanders are the better team.

5.

Climbing to the Top

I t snowed early Thursday, April 14. While the afternoon was clear, the temperature was still very chilly. Yet, 15,840 people left their jobs and homes for Hilltop Park to see the New York Highlanders open their 154-game season—increased from the previous 140—against the World Series Champion Boston Pilgrims. Six thousand of the fans who filed through the 165th Street gates could find individual seats in the covered grandstand. The other 10,000 just fit into the space available in the open bleachers down the right field line and the partly protected stands down the left field line. Those who found themselves in the upper rows in the vicinity of home plate had the added benefit of an unobstructed view of the Hudson River and the New Jersey Palisades.

On this day, each person who entered the park was given a small American flag, which, like the larger version on the grandstand, snapped and flared in the strong wind that drove across the Hudson from the Jersey shore. Although the game was to start at three-thirty, people began streaming in two hours early. The Hilltop was all decked out in bunting and banners. At three o'clock, preceded by the 69th Regiment Band, the players of both clubs marched shoulder to shoulder, in the customary opening day manner, from the clubhouse in center field to their roofed benches. The brand-new uniforms they wore had a high collar and half or three-quarter sleeve, and were made of baggy eight-ounce flannel. Since they shrunk in the laundry, players had to begin the year with shirts and pants a full size too large. While their uniforms billowed around their bodies, their hats, with their tight little crown and short, round brim, barely stood away from their heads. Waiting for Clark Griffith were floral arrangements in the shape of a horseshoe and crossed bats. The manager was instructed to stick his head through the horseshoe, which he finally did after some initial reluctance. Finally, with a large number of dignitaries and old "Cap" Anson looking on, former Judge Olcott threw out the first ball and game time was just minutes away.

After the starting batteries were announced by megaphone and the Highlanders took the field, Boston Pilgrim lead-off hitter Patsy Dougherty stepped toward the plate. There was no set pregame drill for teams at this time. Loosening up, including hitting, was a casual affair done in front of the stands with no screen or cage. If Dougherty had not arranged for a few practice strokes before his first at-bat, he might have been walking up there cold. As the Boston left fielder was about to get set in the batter's box, everything mysteriously stopped and everyone stood still. "Then came a spectacle unusual for baseball grounds," reported *The New York Times*. "The band played the 'Star Spangled Banner' and instantly every occupant of the seats arose and remained standing until the band ceased playing." As Dougherty moved back toward the plate, he could look down both foul lines and see a novel situation. Heretofore, a team was allowed only one coach, except if two or more base runners were on. But this season, coaches at third and first were permitted at all times. Furthermore, if Dougherty fouled off a pitch, providing he didn't have two strikes on him, it would be counted as a strike. The National League had adopted this "foul-strike rule" in 1901; the American League in 1903. It was a highly controversial alteration in the regulations, and many of the game's players, writers, and fans thought it very damaging. A critic in *Sporting Life,* for instance, complained that "the public . . . does not pay its good money to see a sport conducted almost wholly in the interest of two individuals—the over-mastering pitcher and the autocratic umpire."

At the Hilltop, as in most parks, there were no spectator seats in center field. Beyond the normally positioned infielders and outfielders, the only shapes observable from the plate were the advertisements posted on the far-off fences. So distant were these wooden walls that companies confidently offered a prize to any strong boy who could hit their ad on a fly. Typically, the American Tobacco Company awarded fifty dollars for a drive that creased its Bull Durham sign, which was displayed in practically every park in the majors. The sign at the Hilltop was big enough, with the bull's head sticking up twice the height of the rest of the fence.

The pitcher whom Dougherty and his teammates faced, across the dirt path in the infield grass that connected the mound and the home plate area, was Jack Chesbro, New York's spitballing ace. "Chesbro was a very busy personage in the opening inning," wrote the *New York Herald.* "He was so full of speed that he couldn't have worked a change of pace if he wanted to." After easily handling Boston's first offensive challenge, the Highlanders got their licks—and what a treat for the frozen hometown fans. In the bottom of the first, New York scored five times off Denton True Young, the famed "Farmer" from Gilmore, Ohio. They called him "Cy" because his fastball was cyclonelike and had been so for fourteen years. In every one of these campaigns except the first, he had won at least 20 games, and five times at least 32—378 in total. For the first three years of the American League's existence, he led in wins (33, 32, and 28); and, for the last two years, he led in complete games and innings pitched. He was a wily veteran who could throw strikes, it seemed, forever. "Young's secret was control," notes Lee Allen. "His control was so unerring and he was so tireless that he just kept throwing as if he were systematically chopping down a tree." But sometimes control pitchers, even great ones, suffer at the hands of pumped-up hitters who dig in with serious purpose. Such was the case on this opening day, and so the Highlanders kept putting runs up on the scoreboard. The one that thrilled the Hilltop crowd the most came in the bottom of the second, when Chesbro, a .185 hitter in 1903, blasted the first ball thrown to him into deep center. As it rolled as far as the fence's stone foundation, "Happy Jack" circled the bases for a solo home run. A third or more of all home runs hit in those days were inside-the-park footraces. Altogether, the Highlanders made their 10 hits count for 8 runs while the Pilgrims could make their 6 hits translate into only 2 runs—the result of home runs by right-fielder John "Buck" Freeman and shortstop Freddy Parent, both inside the park.

As was the custom then, newspapers and saloons would post the local team's score, inning by inning, on bulletin boards, blackboards, or hanging electric scoreboards. The young George "Specs" Toporcer, later an infielder with the St. Louis Cardinals, got a job posting scores for a saloon on the corner of Eighty-fifth Street and First Avenue. "The scores would come in on a Western Union ticker tape, and I'd proudly write them on a large blackboard in the back room of the saloon," recounted Toporcer.

> For this, I got 50 cents and the right to eat whatever free lunch was on the counter. . . . Naturally, this job made me the envy of all the kids in the neigh-

borhood. Dozens of them crowded outside the saloon when I was posting the scores. . . . As I wrote the scores, those on the ledge would shout them down to the kids below. One of them always chalked the scores on the sidewalk for the benefit of people passing by.

The message pinned, chalked, and lit where New Yorkers gathered Thursday afternoon happily proclaimed that the brash, upstart Highlanders had beaten the World Champion Pilgrims—and decisively, at that.

While the Hilltop was filled almost to capacity that opening day, another large mass of baseball fans, approximately 15,000, went to see the Giants play the Brooklyn Superbas at Washington Park, near the Gowanus Canal in Red Hook. This field had been the Brooklyn club's home since 1898, when it returned from a trial use of Brownsville's Eastern Park. Driven by poor transportation and the howling winds off Jamaica Bay back to its old, heavily industrialized Irish-tenement neighborhood, the organization built a new park across the street from the one used before. Construction costs were shared by two streetcar lines that passed a block from the grounds, as baseball was good business for them.

The pregame festivities featured the use of a relatively new instrument in New York life—the automobile. Introduced shortly before the turn of the century, the speedy, self-propelled carriage was not seen universally as a blessing. The very first recorded automobile accident took place in New York City on May 30, 1896, when a bicycle rider named Evylyn Thomas was knocked down by Henry Wells driving a Duryea motor car. Miss Thomas was taken to Manhattan Hospital with a broken leg. In 1899, these rapid promotors of mayhem were forbidden in Central Park and a nine-mile-an-hour speed limit was instituted along with a requirement that every vehicle carry a warning gong. Many felt that the city was an inappropriate place for such a freewheeling mode of transportation. Nevertheless, opening day plans to bring the Giants to Washington Park by gasoline-driven autos proceeded. The New York players were escorted by vehicles carrying the Brooklyn players, the Brooklyn Elks, and Shannon's 23rd Regiment Band. When the procession reached the Brooklyn Bridge, according to the *Brooklyn Daily Eagle,* an automobile carrying several Superbas ran into a wagon,

> upsetting the vehicle and knocking down the horses, one of which hung over the edge in imminent danger of falling into the river below. He was rescued with difficulty. Two wheels were knocked off the auto, but the players succeeded in holding on.
> In the meantime, a car came bounding along and was stopped only in the nick of time by the motorman, thereby avoiding a collision and a probable fatality. The players, attired in their uniforms as they were, boarded an elevated train and rode to the grounds, congratulating themselves on having escaped with their lives. There was another collision between two autos and the upshot was that the ball tossers voted to eschew such parades in the future.

By the time the shaken assemblage arrived at Washington Park and the opening day rituals were observed, it was four o'clock and a severe chill had set in. Right fielder George Browne heated things up a little for Giant fans by smacking a lead-off single to center. At this point, Bob Emslie, the lone umpire, moved behind the mound so that he could keep an eye on the runner at first while still being in a position to call balls and strikes. When rookie third baseman Art Devlin dropped a sacrifice bunt in front of the plate, Browne went to second. First baseman Dan McGann promptly singled to right, driving in Browne with the Giants' first run of the season, and took second on right fielder Harry Lumley's throw home. The events that took place were an umpire's nightmare, as Sam Crawford, the slugging outfielder for Cincinnati and Detroit, explained:

You know that one umpire just can't see everything at once. . . . He'd be out there behind the pitcher with, say a man on second base, and the batter would get a hit out to right field. Well, the umpire would be watching the ball and the batter rounding first and trying for second. Meanwhile, the guy who was on second would cut third base wide by fifteen feet on his way home. Never came anywhere close to third base, you know. We'd run with one eye on the ball and the other on the umpire!

"You did a lot of running," lamented American League umpire Billy Evans,

and—let's face it—a lot of guessing. Many a time, watching the runners and the ball at the same time—I couldn't watch 'em all—I know some players wouldn't go all the way home at all, but would cut the plate and duck into the dugout. But I could never quite catch them, so what could I do.

Clean-up hitter "Sandow" Mertes, Giant left fielder, followed with another single to right, and the score was a quick 2–0. Brooklyn got one back in the bottom of the first, but that was the only run Christy Mathewson allowed them this day. Gutted by American League raids, the former champions of the American Association in 1899 and the National League in 1900 could no longer live up to their nickname, the Superbas or proud ones. They began using this characterization after manager Ned Hanlon and a number of Oriole stars were transferred by the Baltimore-Brooklyn syndicate that owned both clubs. It referred to their new outlook and put to advantage the popularity of a talented acrobatic act that happened to be called "Hanlon's Superbas." By 1904, their outlook had changed, and the four errors they made in this game against the Giants indicated little similarity between their ball club and anything acrobatic. The final score was a lopsided 7–1, an auspicious beginning for McGraw's pennant-hopeful New Yorkers.

Considering the wintry weather conditions, owners of all the Greater New York clubs had to be pleased with opening day attendance. The preseason American League protest concerning the splitting of the metropolitan baseball crowd did not seem to be based on an accurate appraisal of the enormous drawing power the game had in this populous and active market.

On the subject of attendance, there was a source of revenue available for any Greater New York organization successful in braving the storms of some public protest and, likely, legal action. Working-class New Yorkers were busy with their jobs during the week and on Saturdays. Sunday, they were off. But New York had a "blue law," as did other eastern states, which prohibited professional entertainment on the seventh day of the week. It is true that despite the law, semi-professional baseball was played on Sunday in upstate New York, and the Sabbath ban was not pressed against minor league teams in Albany, Schenectady, Syracuse, or Utica. However, New York City was another matter. Here the Sabbatarians—those who believed in strict observance of the Sabbath—tended to be more vigilant. Their terrible fear was that the large immigrant, non-Protestant population would be unleashed by a lenient attitude toward the blue law and begin altering habits and practices that they saw as essentially American. Testing the waters after the 1903 season, the Giants played a benefit game against a semi-pro team on a Sunday, at Olympic Field, 136th Street and Fifth Avenue, in Harlem. A crowd of 7,000 bought 25-cent scorecards instead of the usual admission tickets that would have definitely made this a professional event, and no interruption by the police occurred. Before the 1904 season began, Charley Ebbets, owner of the Brooklyn Superbas, announced that his team was scheduling Sunday games in Washington Park.

The first of these, against the Boston Beaneaters on April 17, was attended by 12,000 spectators who bought 25-, 50- and 75-cent scorecards corresponding to the different prices for seats.

Since at no time was there any sign of police objection, it was assumed, after the game, that the time had come for Sunday baseball in Greater New York. Although John Brush had "long been opposed to [Sunday baseball], believing it to have an injurious effect on the game," he decided that "if the public demands Sunday games the demand should be met, so long as this can be done without violating the law." A spokesman for the Highlanders thought that his club would also play on the Sabbath, even though a clause in the Hilltop lease prohibited such a schedule. Then, on April 24, the issue became more complex. After two pitches had been thrown in a Sunday game at Washington Park between the Superbas and the Philadelphia Phillies, the police walked onto the field and arrested the pitcher, catcher, and lead-off hitter. Baseball played on the Sabbath in Greater New York would now be ruled on by the courts.

By early May, the Highlanders, fluctuating in the standings between second and fourth place, were looking to strengthen their club a bit. The man they wanted was Albert "Kip" Selbach, an eleven-year veteran outfielder who was a regular .300 hitter. Selbach belonged to the hapless Washington Senators, destined for last place in the American League. The deal, as the newspapers had it, was Selbach and veteran catcher Malachi Kittredge for the Highlanders' John Anderson and rookie catcher Monte Beville. The press saw this swap as an absolute steal for New York. The problem was that Patsy Donovan, former Cardinal and Pirate manager, who just then took over the leadership of the Senators, saw things the same way and informed the angry Highlander owner, Frank Farrell, that the trade was off. The only transaction that came out of the New York-Washington talks was the purchase, by the Highlanders, of utility player "Bullet Jack" Thoney.

So, on May 11, when the third-place Highlanders hosted the fifth-place Cleveland Blues, "Honest John" Anderson ran out as the starting left fielder and Jack Thoney took the injured William "Wid" Conroy's third base position. Called the Blues because they wore the traditional blue uniforms associated with the old National League franchise, this Cleveland team (later the Indians) had the hitting and physical style of play to make opponents "blue" as well. With the Blues came one of baseball's finest players and attractions: Napoleon "Larry" Lajoie, the smooth and powerful "Frenchman" from the cotton mill town of Woonsocket, Rhode Island. Lajoie—he pronounced it "Laj-a-way"—was one of the great prizes captured by the American League during the "Great Baseball War." In 1901, his first year in the new major circuit, he hit .422, a figure that led not only all American League hitters that season but all American League hitters in every succeeding season as well. The 1904 season was his ninth in the majors, and, thus far, he had never hit lower than .328. "Big Ed" Walsh, the Chicago White Sox's husky spitballer, grumbled, "If you pitched inside to him, he'd tear a hand off the third baseman, and if you pitched outside, he'd knock down the second baseman." "Kid" Nichols called him "the hardest hitter I ever pitched to. He used to hit on a line with terrific momentum." And he was also one of the surest defensive second basemen of his day. Although not particularly fast, notes Lee Allen, "he wasted no motion scooping up balls with perfect grace, as if in a dream." All in all, thought Tim Murnane, *Boston Globe* writer and pioneer first baseman in the very early days of the National League, "Lajoie is the grandest ballplayer the game has ever produced. He is the ideal size for a player [6 feet 1 inch, 195 pounds], has a fine reach, is strong in every limb, has a keen eye, is aggressive, and has no weakness. As a hitter, he is unrivaled." And all of this talent belonged to a man whose profile might have earned him fame as a matinee idol.

Lajoie's habitual hard play was what New York fans saw too much of during the mid-May series at Hilltop Park. In the first game, Willie Keeler was Lajoie's victim. "Wee Willie" singled to lead off the bottom of the first, and when Dave Fultz popped up a bunt to the right of pitcher "Strawberry Bill" Bernhardt, Keeler started toward second and then turned back to first. At the same time, Lajoie raced in to grab the ball and collided with Keeler. Umpire Charley "Silver" King called Keeler out for interference. The little Highlander was noticeably dazed by Lajoie's jolt but had enough breath and spirit left to argue the call, whereupon he was ejected from the game. The Highlanders won this opener, 4–3, thanks to a two-run homer by "Kid" Elberfeld to deep center and two run-producing singles by "Deacon" McGuire. The next day, it was Elberfeld's turn to suffer the effects of Lajoie's hustle. When the Blues' second baseman tried to stretch a single to right into a double, Elberfeld covered second. "King Larry" came barreling in and caught the previous day's hero with his spikes. Elberfeld was forced to leave the game, which turned out to be a 7–0 Cleveland victory. Jack Chesbro had a miserable time of it, giving up 13 hits and dropping his record to a disappointing 4–3. Fortunately for New York, Jack Powell held on to win a 7–6 decision in the third game, and Chesbro returned after just a day's rest to win 10–1, on the last day of the series. Capturing three out of four games gave the Highlanders a 13–8 record and a tie with the Athletics for second place. Ahead of both were the 18–5 Pilgrims.

The Giants, in early May, were in first place in the National League. They had started fast and, already, were not at all appreciated on the road, especially McGraw. Grantland Rice wrote that "his very walk across the field in a hostile town was a challenge to the multitude." *Sporting Life* reported the existence of an "anti-McGraw league in St. Louis whose members are pledged not to attend games when the Giants play in St. Louis." However, on Saturday, May 7, 7,820 people were willing to pay to see McGraw and the Giants do battle with the fifth-place hometown Cardinals. At the end of eight innings, this good-size crowd had to have been pleased with its decision, as St. Louis led, 1–0, in a very well played contest. In the top of the ninth, Giant catcher Jack Warner singled for the fourth hit off right-hander Jack Taylor. McGraw then put himself in as a pinch runner. When Roger Bresnahan successfully pinch-hit for pitcher Luther Taylor, McGraw crossed the plate with, as *The New York Times* saw it, "nearly every member of the visiting team siding him." Billy Gilbert, coaching first as well as playing second for the Giants since the hiring of special coaches was not yet the practice, and being "more enthusiastic than the rest, followed his manager around the bases from first. As McGraw was nearing third, one of the team dashed to the plate, while the rest stood howling on third base." When Cardinal first baseman "Eagle Eye" Jake Beckley, a seventeen-year veteran and team captain, went to complain to field umpire Gus Moran—on occasion two umpires were assigned to one game—"another New York player dashed for the plate from the coaching line. Beckley, thinking Bresnahan had made the dash, tossed the ball toward home plate, with no one covering the position, and Bresnahan scored." St. Louis manager Charley "Kid" Nichols ran over to home plate umpire Jimmy Johnstone and argued that Gilbert and the Giant players who left their bench had violated Section 17 of Rule 56, which stated:

> If one or more members of the team at bat stand or collect at or around a base for which a base runner is trying, thereby confusing the fielding side and adding to the difficulty of making such play, the base runner shall be declared out for the interference of his teammate or teammates.

When Johnstone rejected Nichols' view, the Cardinal leader

lodged a formal protest over what turned out to be the winning run. But this was not yet the day of strict adherence to the fine points of the rule book. Baseball was still regarded by most of its participants as a war among rough men who were expected neither to ask for nor give any quarter. Even the press was unsympathetic with the Cardinals' appeal to change the outcome of the afternoon's rough events. *The Sporting News,* for example, brushed right past the juridical aspects of the dispute and charged Beckley with making a doltish play:

> The Giants did invade the field, Gilbert, a coacher, cutting across the diamond from first to third base, some of them collecting around third base and others at the plate, but no confusion was created in the minds of the Cardinals, nor were they prevented from making a play at either base for the reason that there was no possible play at either point until Beckley lost his head and hurled the ball homeward. . . . The plain, unvarnished facts are that the Giants tied the game by batting and Beckley threw it away by stupidity.

When National League President Pulliam announced that he had rejected Nichols' protest, the McGravians officially won another game, and Beckley added an embarrassing anecdote to his lengthy career that he would forever have to explain to unsympathetic ears.

After the St. Louis game featuring Jake Beckley's "error," the Giants began to struggle. For two weeks, a simple pattern developed: either McGinnity pitched and won or the New Yorkers lost. Even Mathewson lost four decisions, the last on May 20 to the Chicago Colts, who, along with the Cincinnati Reds, had brushed by the Giants in the standings. Furthermore, during the open carriage ride back to the hotel, the frustrated New Yorkers were surrounded by what the *New*

York Herald called "howling fanatics, who seriously threatened to injure some of the visiting players. . . . Christy Mathewson was derided for his defeat, and the shouts of the fans were somewhat more expressive than the star twirler cared to listen to."

The Giants returned to the Greater New York area on May 24. Still in third place, two games back of Cincinnati, they looked forward to a five-game series with sixth-place Brooklyn and a chance "to get well." The two teams had played five times before, with the Manhattan club taking four of them. The rivalry had always been and would always be intense. Frank Graham tells the story of the kindly old Brooklyn priest who saw too many of these bitter contests and erupted, one night, with the admission, "I hate the Giants!" The series opened in Washington Park, with the visitors sending out McGinnity against the home team's Bill Reidy. A large weekday crowd of 6,000 cheered the Superbas' good fortune through the first two innings as 3 walks, 3 hits, and a McGinnity throwing error gave Brooklyn a 3–0 lead. But the Giants answered with 3 runs in the third and 1 more in each of the next two innings for a 5–3 final score. The "Iron Man" had been nearly perfect from the third inning on, facing only 23 hitters. In form, it was a vintage McGinnity performance as the Superbas hit pop-up after pop-up. The submarine curve ball artist ran his personal record to a sensational 11–0.

The Polo Grounds was to be the scene of the next three battles. In the first of these, the Superbas again started off well, building another early 3-run lead. This time the Brooklyn pitcher, Oscar "Flip Flap" Jones, held on until the seventh before the Giant bats began to respond. In the top of the ninth, with the score now 4–4, Jack Cronin, in relief of the spent Jones, walked Dan McGann, who then reached second on Mertes's groundout. "Moose" McCormick hit one wide of first, forcing Frank "Pop" Dillon to field the ball and throw it to Cronin, who was covering the bag. But Cronin let the throw get away and McGann turned third and kept coming, scoring the run that ultimately gave the Giants the game, 5–4. McGann's running ability was the greatest part of the story in the third game, too. Five times he attempted to steal on Brooklyn catcher Lou "Old Dog" Ritter, and five times he was successful. No one in the history of the National League, since 1900, has exceeded this total in a single game. The *New York Herald,* searching for an explanation, thought he had to have "borrowed the winged foot of Mercury for this occasion" and likened him to one of those daring and elusive Japanese patrols that was destroying Russian forces in the one-sided war then raging in the Far East. Mathewson, returning to form, earned the win in this 3–1 contest, evening his personal record at 5–5. More important was what this victory did for the club in the standings. The Giants added their 21st win against 10 losses, giving them a tie with Chicago for first place. So tight was this National League race that third-place Cincinnati trailed the Giants and Colts by .001.

As close as the three previous games had been, the fourth, held on Saturday, May 28, was even harder on the nervous system of the players and the large crowd that filled the seats and overflowed behind ropes stretched across the deep outfield. At the end of eight innings, the score was tied, 2–2. The Superbas took the lead with a run in the top of the tenth and were just three outs from a much-needed victory. When Bill Dahlen was called out on strikes, the distance was cut to two outs. Second baseman Billy Gilbert had 2 hits in the game, so Cronin pitched carefully to him. Besides, following Gilbert would be catcher Jack Warner, the Giants' eighth hitter, and then pitcher McGinnity. Still, Cronin was too fine with Gilbert and lost him. Up came Warner, who slammed the first pitch into the bleachers just foul. Those pulling for Brooklyn settled back in their seats with great relief. On the next pitch, the left-hand-hitting Warner found another pitch he could pull, and this time the ball sailed into the short right field stands (258 feet) in fair territory. The Polo Grounds was a madhouse. Warner dashed around the bases with the unreserved public jubilation that few accomplishments besides athletic glory allow. According to the *New York Herald*:

> Men and boys, hatless and coatless some of them, piled over the New York players in a crazy rush to get so much as a touch of the hem of their hero's garment. He was seized by arms and legs and carried for a little until he for a moment fought off adulation with his fists, striking right and left.
>
> Over the heads of the crowd that surged around the white uniformed player, indistinct in the eddying dust, cushions sailed through the air. Men rent their clothing in the madness of the exultation, and cared not a whit what became of the shreds.

Warner's dramatic home run kept McGinnity's winning streak intact—at 12—and kept the Giants tied with the Colts for first place.

Since the courts had not yet issued a decision on the matter of baseball and the blue law, the fifth and final game of the New York-Brooklyn series was to be played on Sunday, May 29, at Washington Park. No Sunday baseball was being planned for Manhattan because the New York City Police Department took the position that the different nature of the neighborhoods around the ballparks made their Sabbath situation different. Washington Park was somewhat isolated from private residences and surrounded by large vacant spaces and factories that were closed on Sunday. In Manhattan, said Police Commissioner McAdoo,

> the neighborhoods are thickly populated and the traffic arrangements for handling large crowds on Sun-

day afternoons might possibly create confusion and annoyance. I would, therefore, at present, be opposed to allowing match games of baseball to be played on Sunday at either of the [Manhattan] parks, which from the nature of the contests would attract large audiences.

On Saturday, May 28, several associations of ministers visited all the local officials, demanding that this planned violation of the Sabbath and the law not be permitted to take place. Deputy Police Commissioner Farrell issued a statement refusing their demand. There would be 15,000 or more people at the field. "If an attempt was made to prevent the game," he stated, "there might be a serious riot." He suggested that the Sabbatarians send witnesses to the game, obtain what evidence there was regarding the violation of the law, and submit their findings to the police. When the expected 15,000 fans, including the Sabbatarian note takers, arrived at Washington Park, they, as before, walked past the ticket booths but were strongly invited to purchase scorecards before going through the turnstiles and taking their seats. It was clear from the cheering that a significant part of this large Sunday crowd came over from Manhattan to see their team complete a five-game sweep. Anticipating a huge turnout, the Brooklyn management had already stretched a rope across a portion of the outfield and, therefore, a ground rule had to be instituted—in this case, making any ball hit beyond the rope an automatic triple. The visitors wasted no time at all, jumping on Brooklyn starter Ed Poole. George Browne singled to left to begin the game and then scored on Art Devlin's ground-rule triple to left. Devlin then scored on "Moose" McCormick's sharp single, also to left. While the Giants continued to add to their run total, their pitcher, George "Hooks" Wiltse, making his first major league start, held off the Superbas with little difficulty. The final score was 7–3. In addition to pitching so well, the very poised young left-hander got two hits. With Chicago also winning, New York clung to a share of first place.

The third-place Highlanders began the month of June in Detroit with Jack Chesbro defeating the seventh-place Tigers, 5–3. Chesbro was a hot pitcher. He had won his previous five games, throwing 2 shutouts and giving up only 4 runs in all. This triumph over the Tigers moved his record up to 10–3. Playing center field for the injured Dave Fultz was Orth "Buck" Collins, just purchased from Rochester. Collins was taking the roster spot of little-used Bob Unglaub, who had to undergo an operation for blood poisoning. "Wid" Conroy was back, but Griffith had to shift him to short to replace "Kid" Elberfeld, another injured regular. This crippled New York attack was led, as usual, by Willie Keeler, with 4 hits. The following day, manager Griffith took things into his own hands. When Detroit got to Ambrose Puttman for 3 runs in the third and another in the fourth, Griffith inserted himself in the game. He had not pitched lately because of an injured right hand sustained while slugging a photographer in Philadelphia. But, then again, his effectiveness depended more upon his head than his hand. "Cy" Young called Griffith a "dinky-dinky pitcher. He didn't have anything but he had a lot of nothing, if you get what I mean. He was smart, though, and he was good at mixing 'em up." "The Old Fox" could handle a bat, too, leading off the Highlanders' key 3-run inning with a bunt single. When the Tigers went down in order in the last of the ninth, the patched-up, pieced-together New Yorkers had a 5–4 win. After dropping the third game, 5–4, Griffith's struggling crew came back behind workhorse Jack Chesbro, who won his 7th in a row with a neat 5–1 five-hitter. But taking three out of four from Detroit left them in third place, trailing Boston by 4½ games and Cleveland by percentage points. The Highlanders had to get their regular line-up back from the infirmary and, if they could, add some talent to make a move on the Pilgrims.

Adding talent, of course, is what all organizations would like to do, and the player virtually all organizations were eying was Walter Clarkson of Harvard College. Clarkson was, according to the *New York Herald*, "one of the finest pitchers that ever took part in a college game." Little wonder—he was the brother of two former major league pitchers: John Clarkson and Arthur "Dad" Clarkson. John, a great star with the National League Chicago White Stockings and Boston Beaneaters in the 1880s and 1890s, had a 326–177 record over twelve seasons. "Dad's" statistics were much less impressive. Walter, seventeen years younger than John and twelve years younger than "Dad," seemed headed for a career as great as his eldest brother's. In fact, the *New York World* reported that "many are of the opinion that Walter is even better than John was at this age." Willie Keeler, who helped coach the Harvard varsity before spring training began—as did teammate Jack Chesbro—said that Walter "had everything" and that he possessed a remarkable supply of baseball brains of the caliber that made John Clarkson so effective. Keeler thought the young right-hander could hold his own in either of the big leagues. For the last two years, Clarkson was chased by the pros but refused to leave Harvard. Now, in the spring of his senior year, he decided to sign with the team for which Keeler and Chesbro played. Apparently, Clarkson planned to keep his professional status a secret until after the college season ended. However, the Harvard Athletic Committee discovered that not only had the school's ace pitcher signed a big league contract with the Highlanders, but he had already accepted money in the form of a bonus. The committee reacted immediately by banning Clarkson from any further participation in college athletics. "Foolish boy," commented *Sporting Life*, "he could have waited to sign professionally for two weeks, couldn't he?"

In the second week of June, the Giants and the Colts, separated by a half-game New York advantage, squared off in the Polo Grounds for a three-game series that meant first place, one way or the other. The pitchers for the first game, on June 10, were to be Mathewson and Mordecai Peter Centennial "Miner" "Three-Finger" Brown. Brown got the first of his many names from the Old Testament, the second from the New Testament, and the third from the fact that he was born the year the United States celebrated its 100th birthday. His nicknames came from his coal-mining hometown, Nyesville, Indiana, and from the results of an accident he had when he was seven years old. While visiting his uncle's farm, Brown put his right hand in a corn grinder, losing much of his right index finger and disfiguring his middle finger. This misfortune turned out, at least in terms of his baseball career, to have been a blessing in a very ugly disguise because Brown's necessarily unconventional grip caused tremendous spin from his thumb and made his curve drop away acutely. He had come to the Colts in a mysterious transaction with St. Louis the previous winter. Brown had only a 9–13 record in his rookie year with the Cardinals. The player for whom he was traded was Jack Taylor, a proven pitcher who had been with the Colts since 1898. For the past two seasons, Taylor had records of 22–11 and 21–14 and had started and completed 33 games in each. Why Brown should be pitching for Chicago instead of Taylor, correctly described by W. A. Phelon in *Sporting Life* as "one of the best in the land," was unclear at this point in the year. Later, the answer would be revealed as part of a disgraceful set of circumstances that had a serious effect on the course of the 1904 season.

A nice-size weekday crowd of 5,000 appeared this Friday afternoon and watched "Matty" make what "Three-Finger" Brown called his "lordly entrance." "He'd wait until about ten minutes before game time," Brown explained, "then he'd come from the clubhouse across the field in a long linen duster like auto drivers wore in those days, and at every step the crowd would yell louder and louder." "Matty's" early season slump was over. Since May 20, when his record was 4–5, he had pitched and won four strong games. Now, confidence restored, he strutted that tall, ruggedly handsome, and slightly self-righteous presence before a worshipful home crowd for the opening game in the series McGraw told the press was "critical . . . in the pennant race." The mild contempt Mathewson seemed to have for his fellow man appeared well deserved today. When it was all over, Chicago catcher "Noisy Johnny" Kling's fourth-inning single was the only hit "Matty" had permitted in a masterful 5–0 victory.

June 11 was a Saturday and an incredible 38,805 showed up, convinced the Giants were on their way to the pennant. So many people descended from the El or stepped out of carriages, which were parked in the roped-off capacious center field section of the bathtub-shaped Polo Grounds, that four times the usual number of police were on hand. No one was permitted on the field until the stands were totally filled, and then the overflow was directed to planking laid outside the diamond and around the outfield. Out in the bleachers, some clung to the slatting that rose behind to cut the view of those outside on the viaduct. Better than the viaduct for a free glimpse of the game was rocky Coogan's Bluff, behind the home plate area of the grandstand. There those who could negotiate the hillside, with or without the help of the grotesque trees scattered about, could peer through the open space below the roof and see a portion of the playing field. Joe McGinnity would be seeking his 15th victory in a row. The all-time record was 19, held by Tim Keefe, also of the Giants, back in 1888; but the "Iron Man" had surpassed Jack Chesbro's 1902 streak of 12 for the Pirates and was establishing a mark for the era begun by the joint operation of the National and American leagues. Bob Wicker would be the Chicago pitcher this day. McGinnity was his usual brilliant self, shutting the Colts out through the regulation nine and two additional innings. Then, in the twelfth, Frank Chance, "the Peerless Leader," led off with a single to right, just by first baseman McGann. When Kling stepped up, Chance looked across and put on the hit-and-run. "Noisy Johnny" grounded the next pitch to short for what ordinarily would be a double play; however, Chance, already sliding into second, forced Bill Dahlen to go to first. McGinnity fooled "Kangaroo" Davy Jones and got the "Great Baseball War's" champion league jumper to tap weakly back to the box; but Chance, playing heads-up as always, advanced to third on the play. With two out and a runner on third, Johnny "the Crab" Evers slapped a single into the shortstop hole, scoring the game's first and only run. Wicker, too, had been terrific. In fact, he carried a no-hitter into the tenth, when Mertes blasted one by third. McGinnity's winning streak had been broken, although it had been unbeatable competition, not a bad day, that did it.

Monday's game, the last in the series, was expected to be another monumental battle. Mathewson returned to the mound for the Giants. He would be opposed by Mordecai Brown, "the three fingered prodigy of the Colts' staff," as the *Chicago Daily Tribune* called him. The two right-handers had 24 memorable dogfights over the years, with Brown triumphing in 13 of them, including this, the initial one, 3–2. A superior Colt defense, featuring a 6–4–3 double play from Joe Tinker to Johnny Evers to Frank Chance, was largely responsible for the outcome. Although Tinker and Evers did not speak to each other through most of their careers, due originally to a fight over a carriage to the ballpark, their fame, along with Chance's, was linked and immortalized by Franklin P. Adams in a poem appearing in the *New York Globe:*

> These are the saddest of possible words,
> Tinker-to-Evers-to-Chance.
> Trio of Bear Cubs fleeter than birds,

Tinker-to-Evers-to-Chance.
Ruthlessly prickling our gonfalon bubble,
Making a Giant hit into a double,
Words that are weighty with nothing but trouble.
Tinker-to-Evers-to-Chance.

The Giants' "gonfalon [pennant] bubble" was not pricked by the Colt victory on this day, but it was blown a little out of reach as New York dropped into second place, a half-game back of Chicago.

On June 19, the Highlanders split a double-header with the St. Louis Browns, while the Pilgrims defeated the White Sox in a single game. What this did for the New Yorkers was move them past Chicago into second place, five games behind Boston. Happy as this news was for Highlander fans, there was still more to celebrate. Their club announced the conclusion of an unbelievable player trade. Patsy Dougherty, a young slugging outfielder, who was a major contributor to the 1903 Boston World Championship, was coming to New York for Bob Unglaub, a first-year infielder, who appeared in just six games, without distinction, before being hospitalized for blood poisoning. Dougherty hit .342 in 1902, the highest average an American League rookie would attain for more than a quarter of a century. The next year, the 6-foot-2, 190-pound even-tempered Irishman hit .331, highest on the Boston club and third in the league. In the 1903 World Series, he banged out 2 home runs and a single in one Pilgrim victory, and 2 ground-rule triples and a single in another. Through the first third of the 1904 season, he had fallen off some, hitting .273, but he was leading all Pilgrims with 10 stolen bases, and there was no reason to suppose he wouldn't catch fire with the bat and top the team for the third straight year. The reaction in Boston was, to say the least, vehement. The *Boston Herald*, among many others, charged that league politics was behind this ridiculous deal:

Manager [Jimmy] Collins simply listened to the importunities of manager Griffith and others to help out New York. New York was in the hole on account of the retirement of outfielder Fultz owing to injuries and it would not do to keep that team in a hole. New York will now have one of the strongest outfields in the country in Anderson, Dougherty and Keeler and with it ought to maintain a leading position in the race.

The idea that the Dougherty-Unglaub trade was made to help strengthen the Highlanders brought National League President Harry Pulliam into the fray. In a statement to the press, Pulliam let loose a major blast at the American League:

> I regret the Dougherty-Unglaub deal very much because . . . it gives credence to the heretofore unjust criticism that professional baseball savors of the hippodrome and is subordinate to the box office.
> Since we have a National Agreement and are affiliated with the American League, we, of necessity, share with it any odium that may attach to it. . . .
> The Boston Club is leading in the race for the pennant, and by their action they deprive themselves of the services of a star outfielder and one of the best hitters in the country. This cannot but weaken their chances for the pennant and strengthen their adversary.
> In this connection I wish to add that no aid will be extended by any club in the National League to the New York club in their fight for the pennant. If they win the fight they must do it by their own efforts, however, the New York club has a valuable asset in the McGraw spirit and in this I think they have a strength that will out-balance any deal made in the past or future, regardless of how many stars are handed to their competitors for the patronage of the baseball public in New York City.

There it was, the agenda so many believed was behind this 1904 season: above all else, capture the New York market for the financial health of the league! New York sportswriter Timothy Sharp jumped on this theme in an article in *The Sporting News*, but he pointed the finger at Pulliam:

> It is patent to every one that Harry has a very soft spot in his heart for Mr. Brush's . . . club, and shows it at every opportunity. The so-called "Giants" get the best of everything, and it would please the National League people to have the McGrawites win the flag. . . . Those big crowds at the Polo Grounds have a hypnotic effect on them and they are willing to do almost anything that will keep them out of jail to get their share of the money. . . . That is why I consider it the height of indiscretion on the part of Pulliam to "butt in" and attempt to besmirch the actions of the Boston Americans and the entire American League in the recent Dougherty-Unglaub trade.

Dougherty joined the Highlanders in time for their June 19 double-header in St. Louis. There he was inserted into the line-up in his customary lead-off spot, moving Keeler down a notch. In the first game, which the Highlanders won, 4–3, Dougherty got 2 hits, including a double; and, in the second game, which the Highlanders lost, 1–0, he doubled again.

For the next series in Washington, Dave Fultz rejoined the Highlander club after a three-week absence; but, as if on some sinister cue, Keeler now had to sit out because of an injury. However, the outfield of Dougherty in left, Fultz in center, and Anderson in right accounted for half of the 8 hits—Dougherty's being a triple—that converted into 3 runs, more than enough to win the first game behind the 4-hit, shutout pitching of Jack Chesbro. Griffith pitched in the second game and won a slugfest, 11–6. New York staged its biggest rally of the season in the fourth inning, scoring seven times. Dougherty began the fun with 1 of the 5 hits he would spray around this afternoon. Jack Powell got the victory on Thursday, 7–4. Dougherty had a hit to keep his consecutive-game hitting streak, as a Highlander, alive at five.

The last stop on the Highlanders' June road trip was Boston. The second-place New York club had narrowed its deficit to 2½ games. Of the seven times Boston and New York went head to head, the latter won four. If the Highlanders could take all of the four contests in this series, they would finish the month on top of the American League. On Saturday, June 25, 16,622 people came out to watch these two fine teams fight it out and to welcome back their former left fielder. "Dougherty received ovation after ovation from the crowd," reported the *New York Herald,* and provided good reason to applaud his return. As the first hitter in the game, he singled to center off "Cy" Young, went to second on Keeler's bunt, moved to third on Wiliams' grounder, and scored on Anderson's fly ball. As he crossed the plate, he took several steps toward the Boston bench, out of force of habit, before he recovered his senses and joined his new teammates. Dougherty later added 2 more hits in what turned out to be a 5–3 Highlander victory, Chesbro's 12th straight. Patsy was pleased. "Yes," he told the press at the Quincy House that evening,

> I suppose you might call this tribute one of the events of the baseball season in Boston, and it is only natural that I should feel gratified. . . . The expression of enthusiasm today demonstrates that the public has a very decided opinion on the matter, and they showed unmistakably on which side their sympathy lies. That is something that any man would appreciate. . . .
>
> I am with a good team now—don't make any mistake about that. I never expect to feel any dissatisfaction on that score.

The struggle between the Highlanders and Pilgrims resumed on Monday, June 27, after a rest on the Sabbath, with Jack Powell and ex-Highlander Jesse Tannehill the pitchers. Once more, Dougherty began the fireworks by singling past shortstop Freddy Parent. When "Buck" Freeman misplayed Keeler's long drive to right, the Highlanders had runners on first and second. After Williams sacrificed both runners over, Anderson delivered a 2-run single. Dougherty later added 2 additional hits, scoring both times and contributing significantly to New York's 8–4 triumph. The Pilgrim's lead had been cut to half a game, with two to play.

The pitchers for the third contest were ex-Pilgrim Tom Hughes and second-year right-hander Norwood Gibson. This time Boston struck first, getting 2 runs thanks largely to a fly ball off the bat of Parent that Dougherty—proving he was still mortal—played into a triple. The newest Highlander star did, however, score the first New York run, in the fourth, after singling his way on. But Gibson allowed the visitors only 5 hits and won, 5–2. Since the last of the four-game set was rained out, June ended with Boston in first by a game and a half.

A third of the season had thus far been played, and the Highlanders had done very well, indeed. They hit well—especially since the acquisition of Patsy Dougherty. They played solidly in the field. And they had the league's most effective pitcher—Jack Chesbro, who was already 16–3. It wouldn't take much, just a little good fortune, for the Highlanders to climb the rest of the way through the next few months to the summit.

After the Colts left the Polo Grounds in mid-June with a half-game lead, they went to Boston and lost two of three. At the same time, the Giants split four games with the Cardinals, and the Reds lost two of three in Brooklyn. The result was that on June 17, just before the Giants and Superbas began a four-game series, New York was in first by a half-game over both Chicago and Cincinnati. As Luther Taylor and Ed Poole got ready for their opening duel before the 2,000 fans who came out to the Polo Grounds this Friday, Ebbets and Hanlon had to be calling on their private sources of good luck to keep the 9–1 New York edge in games from increasing and causing further humiliation. But, even when things went well for Brooklyn, they went better for their Manhattan rivals. Only 2 runs would be scored this day, both in the first inning, and both by the Giants. Bresnahan walked, Browne bunted his way on, Devlin sacrificed, McGann singled to Dobbs (normally an outfielder) at deep short, and Mertes got on through a throwing error by second baseman Jacklitsch (normally a catcher). Poole allowed only 3 more hits the rest of the way, but Taylor allowed only 4 hits himself and his team played strong defensively. On Saturday, 15,000 viewed McGinnity's attempt to break his 2-game losing streak and were not disappointed. The Giants' success, 5–1, moved the "Iron Man's" record to 15–2.

On this same day, a very significant statement was issued by Judge William Jay Gaynor concerning Sabbath baseball in Brooklyn—a matter of immediate concern because the next game in the current series was to be played in Washington Park on Sunday. Gaynor denied a motion for dismissal of the complaints against the arrested ballplayers, stating that the warrants did state facts constituting a crime. His ruling implied that the distinction between the direct charging of admission and the selling of scorecards was no longer being respected. The only material question in the Gaynor courtroom was whether the Sunday gathering was for a private or an advertised professional sporting event.

Nevertheless, on Sunday, June 19, the Giants and Superbas went ahead with their game. Only 6,000 spectators— half, of them *The New York Times* thought, from Manhattan— considered it worth their time to see major leaguers play on Sunday. Since 40,000 came out to see the two St. Louis clubs play double-headers and 24,800 showed up in Chicago to see the Colts host the Beaneaters, this could be taken as a comment on the demoralized spirit of Brooklyn fans. By the end of the game, many of the devout who did make it to Washington Park might have fallen away. "Hooks" Wiltse, making his second start, registered his second win. This time he threw a 3-hit shutout, while his own Giant forces scored 11 runs on 18 hits. Every man in the New York line-up got at least 1 hit, with Browne and Bresnahan getting 4 and 3 respectively.

Since "Matty" was on the hill for the last game back in the Polo Grounds, a sweep seemed imminent. His opposite number was Bill Reidy, who had not won a game this season. A cynic might have said that the Superbas gave every bit of evidence of wanting to keep things this way for Reidy, as they committed 9 errors, including a season's individual record of 5 by ex-Giant shortstop Charley Babb.

This New York-Brooklyn series represented a noteworthy breakthrough in terms of the National League standings. As the Giants inflated their win total by 4, the Colts and Reds were frustrating each other in Cincinnati. By Monday evening, June 20, the Giants had a 2½-game lead over the Reds and a 3-game lead over the Colts. The feel of a tangible lead must have been inspiring to McGraw and his team because they ripped through the rest of the month without a single loss. As of June 28, the New Yorkers had won 12 straight and stretched their lead to 5 games over the Colts and 6 over the Reds.

Everything was going right for Brush and McGraw—except that they might be only one of two champion teams from Manhattan.

6.

Staying at the Top

I n the nineteenth century, few players came out of the college ranks. When Fred Tenney moved straight from Brown College to the Boston Beaneaters, he was quickly dubbed "the Soiled Collegian" and greatly resented. But, by the early twentieth century, college baseball had become a major attraction and its stars were regularly recruited. In fact, in 1904, according to baseball historian-sociologist Steven Riess, one-quarter of the rookies in the major leagues had some college experience. One of these, Walter Clarkson, a recent graduate of Harvard, was ready to make his long-awaited debut with the New York Highlanders on Saturday, July 2, in the first game of a double-header against the Washington Senators. Opposing Clarkson would be Jack Townsend. Eight thousand people came to the Hilltop to see the former Harvard ace pitch, and, in terms of his personal performance, he did not disappoint them. They saw a slim, 5-foot-10 right-hander, who relied on a drop and a change-up, limit the Senators to 8 hits. "He has an easy and rather pleasing delivery," said *The New York*

Times, "and at critical moments . . . showed the nerve of a veteran." The *New York Herald* commented that "his work in the box was such as would win nine games out of ten." Unfortunately, the Highlanders got only 4 hits and 2 runs off Townsend, 1 run short of the Senators' total, and Clarkson broke into the big leagues with a loss.

Nevertheless, all the additional pitching help the Highlanders could get would be greatly welcomed later that week, when the Philadelphia Athletics came in for a four-game set, including a July 4 double-header, with their three extremely tough hurlers: "Gettysburg Eddie" Plank, Albert "Chief" Bender, and Eddie "Rube" Waddell. Not only did these three represent the finest overall pitching staff in the American League, but they also represented an example of the incredibly wide spectrum of personalities that could be found in turn-of-the-century major league baseball. Plank, the most productive left-hander in American League history, was a college-educated (Gettysburg College), deliberate, and meticulous individual on and off the field. He was the epitome of the intellectual pitcher. He never beat himself with walks in crucial situations and could drive hitters crazy with tantalizing tosses just off the corners of the plate. Bender, a tall right-hander of German-Dutch-Chippewa descent (hence, "Chief"), was one of the most open and good-natured people in the game. He kept a bag of talcum powder in his back pocket and rubbed it on the ball, making it dart downward out of reach. All of his pitches were delivered after he kicked his left leg so high in the air that the hitter had to wonder what happened to the ball and when it would be coming. And then there was Waddell. "Boy, there was one of a kind," said former teammate Sam Crawford, with the mixture of respect and bewilderment everyone used when trying to explain this extraordinary eccentric.

They never made another like him. . . . He'd pitch one day and we wouldn't see him for three or four days after. He'd just disappear, go fishing or something, or be off playing ball with a bunch of twelve-year olds in an empty lot somewhere. . . .

The main thing you had to watch out for was not to get him mad. If things were going smoothly and everyone was happy, Rube would be happy too, and he'd just go along, sort of half-pitching. Just fooling around, lackadaisical, you know. But if you got him mad, he'd really bear down, and then you wouldn't have a chance. Not a chance.

They called Waddell "Rube" because of his rural Pennsylvania background and his stereotypic farm boy ingenuousness, but he could fire those southpaw fastballs as hard as anyone who ever toed a rubber. Tommy Leach admitted that sometimes when he was supposed to be guarding third, he would lose his concentration: "I wasn't playing, I was watching! 'How can a man throw that hard?' I used to wonder to myself. He had a terrific curve ball too, and great control." "Cy" Young thought Waddell was the greatest pitcher of all time. But the Athletics didn't have the hitting to match their truly fine pitching, and the Highlanders swept the series, beating Plank, Bender, and Waddell in close games to stay within reach of the Pilgrims, who had just swept the Senators.

Walter Clarkson might have gotten the attention of the press as a potentially important player added to the roster of a contending club, but the alteration that mattered most when the Highlanders and Pilgrims faced each other in their early July confrontation was not the rookie pitcher but the veteran outfielder "Kip" Selbach. Billy "Tip" O'Neill was supposed to fill the flashing spikes of Patsy Dougherty after he was virtually handed to the Highlanders. But the rookie found the spotlight too bright and managed only a .196 batting average in seventeen games. It was evident that he couldn't be counted on to start for the World Champions. So, another one-sided trade took place, this time sending Selbach, the hard-hitting Washington Senator who, ironically, was earlier in the year headed for New York, to Boston for O'Neill. The New York deal was killed by the new Washington manager Patsy Donovan because, in part, he didn't view John Anderson as Selbach's equal. Now, in Billy O'Neill, he would get very much less. But it wasn't the Senators who were the biggest losers—they could finish last without Selbach; it was the Highlanders. Boston, the club they were trying to jimmy out of first place, had regained a large portion of the offense it lost in Dougherty. American League officials must have had a trying week calculating what all this looked like and what kind of an effect it would have on the pennant race.

When the American League's two best teams met in New York in early July, Selbach made his presence felt right away by driving in 3 runs in Boston's 4–1 first game victory; getting 2 hits, including a triple, in Boston's 12–3 second game victory; and sacrificing the winning run into scoring position in Boston's 2–1 third game victory. Jack Chesbro was the pitching victim in the first and third games, ending his personal winning streak at 14—tying the season's high mark set earlier by Joe McGinnity. The fourth game went to New York, 10–1. In this one, Selbach was kept in check; Dougherty, however, had 4 of the Highlanders' 17 hits, including a triple. As of July 11, when this Boston-New York series was concluded, the Pilgrims held on to a 2½-game lead.

The Giants ended June with their 14th consecutive team victory and opened July, at home, in the middle of a series with Boston. The Beaneaters were afflicted with New York's 15th and 16th straight triumphs during the first days of the new month. When, after Sunday, the schedule resumed, McGraw's men welcomed the last-place Philadelphia Phillies for a July 4 double-header. Ten thousand came for the morning game and saw Taylor win, 4–1, for his 5th and the team's 17th in a row. Twenty-two thousand then watched Mathewson win the afternoon end of the set, 11–3, for his 5th and the team's 18th in a row. Their string of victories now equalled the one established by the 1885 Chicago White Stockings and the 1894 Baltimore Orioles. The record, 20, held by the 1884 Providence Grays, could be tied by a sweep of the Phillies, but this would have to be accomplished in Philadelphia's Huntington Park, as the series abruptly switched sites. Things looked good for the Giants, however, as McGinnity was sent out against "Frosty Bill" Duggleby, a five-year veteran right-hander who had only one winning season and early exits in his last two starts. For five and a half innings, the small crowd of 2,000 suffered through the accretion of a 4–1 Giant lead. But, in the bottom of the sixth, the Phillies struck back for 3 runs to tie, and, in the next inning, added a fifth score to take the lead. Nevertheless, as if they had a compact with destiny, the Giants got the run they needed to draw even in the ninth. Phillie rooters must have steeled themselves for their team's 11th loss in 13 meetings with the New Yorkers. One of the fascinating possibilities in this game of many parts then manifested itself: sometimes a scratch hit by the weakest player can reverse the apparent direction of fortune and thwart the toughest of opponents. In the bottom of the tenth, with Taylor relieving McGinnity, catcher Charley "Red" Dooin singled and moved to second on rookie left fielder Sherry Magee's roller to first. Up came rookie utility infielder Bob Hall, struggling with a batting average under .200. Taylor fooled him into hitting only a small portion of the ball in the direction of shortstop Dahlen. The little pop-up drifted just beyond "Bad Bill" and just before the charging outfielders "Sandow" Mertes and Roger Bresnahan. Dooin bolted for home and the Giants' winning streak came to a sudden and maddening end.

The next day, as if fate had made its point and was now taunting the Giants, Mathewson had no trouble holding the Phillies scoreless for eight innings while his team crossed the plate twelve times. After "Red" Ames gave up 3 runs in the ninth, the final 12–3 count could be regarded only as a nice fresh start instead of what it might have been: a record-tying 20th consecutive victory. Still, a record of 19 of the last 20 was sensational and so swelled the New York figures in the standings that Chicago fell 10 games back; Cincinnati, 11½ games. The sight of a league championship flag flying atop the Polo Grounds was taking firm shape in the mind's eye of the Giants and their rooters.

It was at the beginning of July that the issue of Sunday ball in Greater New York was settled for 1904 and the foreseeable future. Police Commissioner McAdoo issued instructions to his department based on Judge Gaynor's interpretation of what constituted a violation of the blue law:

> If a game of baseball is played in either the Borough of Brooklyn or the Borough of Queens on next Sunday and the game is a public exhibition, to which the public is invited by advertisement or otherwise and for which an admission fee is charged, the police must arrest all the offenders.

"All the offenders" is the phrase that had to leap out at Charley Ebbets. This included players, umpires, scorecard sellers—and perhaps club officials. Ebbets had planned a game at Washington Park against the Phillies on Sunday, July 3, but McAdoo's threat changed all that. Besides, attendance at these Sabbath spectacles in Brooklyn, going nowhere in the standings, had dwindled to the point at which financial benefit was no longer a serious factor. Therefore, Ebbets announced to the press that Sunday's game was off and that such contests would not be held at Washington Park for the rest of the year.

By the third week of July, the Highlanders were trailing the Pilgrims by 3½ games and beginning to get anxious at the short distance between the teams that they couldn't seem to close. Right before a big series with the third-place White Sox, Griffith swung a deal with the Senators for right-handed pitcher Al Orth (3–4), giving up "Long Tom" Hughes (7–11) and Bill Wolfe (0–3). Orth was in his tenth year and had recorded some fine numbers in the past for the Philadelphia Phillies. Unfortunately, Washington had been a rough place to pitch over the last few seasons, as his 10–21 mark in 1903 indicated. This season, Orth had struggled with ill health, at one point losing a substantial amount of weight from his 6-foot, 200-pound stature. But now he was back in shape. Although he didn't have much of a conventional breaking ball, as his nickname "the Curveless Wonder" attested, he did have an effective "thumb ball," or submarine spitter. "The number of 'popups' hit off Orth's pitching," said Johnny Evers, "was one of the wonders of the game, being almost twice the normal. . . ." Revere Rodgers, in *The Sporting News*, called him "one of the most finished and wisest twirlers of today. . . . This good-natured Virginian is about the coolest proposition when toeing the slab that I ever recollect seeing."

The first three games against the White Sox, at the Hilltop, turned out badly for the New Yorkers, allowing Chicago to slip past them into second place. The Highlanders needed a "stopper" and Orth was given the task. Orth's first start in the big city was on a very rainy Monday, July 25, with Frank "Yip" Owen on the hill for the visitors. "As a pitchers' contest and as an exhibition of vigorous and accurate fielding," wrote *The New York Times*, "the last meeting . . . between the Greater New Yorks and the Chicagos has not been surpassed this season by the local clubs of the big leagues. . . ." Both pitchers threw 4-hit shutouts going into the bottom of the ninth. Dougherty led off the last half of the last inning of regulation play with a triple to right—and up stepped Willie Keeler. The small crowd of 1,522 began to buzz, anticipating something exciting from their diminutive hero. Chicago manager-center fielder Fielder (his given name) Jones moved his infield in for a play at the plate. As if keeping pace with the game, the drizzle, which had been a source of irritation all day, picked up in intensity. Jones came running in from the outfield, demanding that the game be stopped. But umpire Jack Sheridan said no and ordered him back to his position. Sheridan was a tall, sturdy, decisive man, who commanded the respect of the players as few of the men in blue did. He was a no-frills guy who, except for the mask, rejected all the devices, such as hidden shin guards and shoe plates, that provided bodily protection. Keeler then swung down on the ball and bounced it through Gus Dundon at shallow second. Dougherty scored and the Highlanders had their sole triumph of the series, 1–0.

Orth's impressive performance aside, the White Sox series gave the Highlander organization cause for worry. There wasn't much margin for error this season in New York and Griffith's job seemed in jeopardy." GRIFFITH TO BE RETIRED?" asked a *New York Times* headline. "It is claimed," the journal stated,

> that Mr. Farrell . . . had become dissatisfied with the management of Clark Griffith, and that he had decided upon a change.
>
> Mr. Farrell, so the story goes, has a very high opinion of [Frank] Selee [of the Chicago Colts] as a manager. He met Selee in New York, it is said, and when the Chicago man was asked whether he would take the management of the Greater New Yorks, he said he would because at that time the pleasantest feelings did not exist between Selee and president [Jim] Hart of the Chicagos. . . .
>
> It is the opinion here that the days of Clark Griffith as manager of the Greater New Yorks are numbered.

Farrell denied that he was looking to get rid of Griffith:

I consider Griffith the best manager in the country, bar none. Griffith has done well as manager of the New Yorks. He has had enough disabled players to drive an ordinary manager to drink, yet his team is third, with a good chance of finishing better than that.

In the end, Selee signed a new contract with the Colts that was to his liking. Colt owner Hart was left with hard feelings about the matter. "While he appreciated the compliment paid to Selee," commented *Sporting Life*, "he did not like [the Highlanders'] method of gunning for talent." Manager Selee, the journal continued, "simply smiled and declared . . . I like Chicago. The people stick with us, winning or losing, and I am going to stick."

Since Selee was going "to stick," he would be around in the fall to lead the Colts on the world tour, in the style of the Spalding journey of 1888–1889, announced by John Brush and Jim Hart. In fact, it was Selee who told the press that ten men would be taken from both the Giants and the Colts to

> play exhibition games in as many of the world's cities as proved practicable. The start may be made in Chicago, playing the first game here, then going to the Pacific Coast by easy stages. A stop will be made in Honolulu, and probably then will follow a voyage to Australia. . . . What players will constitute the ten taken by each team will depend largely on the plans and wishes of the players themselves. . . .

If this world tour took place as planned, neither the Giants nor the Colts could play in the World Series against the winners of the American League pennant. Why Hart was lending his support to the sabotaging of the World Series was not clearly understood at the time. But he seemed to be an angry man and had been so ever since the postseason series between his club and the White Sox in October 1903. Winning the long, fifteen-game cross-city challenge meant a great deal to both these clubs, but more to the older organization that had lost its long-time monopoly on Chicago's hearts and funds. However, it did not appear that Hart had much to worry about. His Colts had the statistical edge in every category, especially the all-important pitching department. The White Sox had a 20-game loser, Patsy Flaherty, but no 20-game winner. The Colts, on the other hand, had three 20-game winners, including Jack Taylor, the proven veteran who finished all but 2 of the 167 games that he started from 1898, his rookie season, through 1903. This was the second year in a row he won 20 games, leading the league in ERA (1.33) and shutouts (8) in 1902.

Naturally, it was Taylor who, on October 1, started the initial game of the 1903 series "for the championship of Chicago," as the *Chicago Sunday Tribune* saw it. And, as could be expected, he won 11–0. All the White Sox could get were 3 hits off the crafty right-hander from Straightville, Ohio. In fact, the Colts won the first three games very easily. Taylor went again in the fourth contest and this time gave up 10 hits, losing 10–9. Three days later he gave up 14 hits, losing 9–3. And, in his fourth appearance in the series, he gave up 11 hits, losing 4–2. After 14 games, the two teams had won 7 games apiece. Since the game scheduled for October 7 had been rained out, the tie breaker would have to be played after October 15, the day the two clubs originally chose to end the series. White Sox owner Charley Comiskey were more than willing to extend the time frame and crown a city champion, but Jim Hart was not. He claimed his decision was based on the expiration of player contracts on October 15. More likely, he did not wish to risk a humiliating Colt defeat. But, there was one more factor in his decision, although it would not be revealed for another year. Hart had lost his commitment to these games because he was convinced that the man he depended upon most, Jack Taylor, was losing deliberately—

for money. This was why, two months after the Colt-White Sox series, Taylor was shipped off to the St. Louis Cardinals for Mordecai "Three-Finger" Brown, who had just completed a less than sterling rookie season. Hart was no longer in favor of postseason interleague play. There was too much prestige on the line for National League teams and too much betting action and room for corruption.

Why the Giant management was arranging for its squad to be in Honolulu and Australia rather than the World Series—and it increasingly appeared the New Yorkers would earn the right to play in it—was partially explained by John McGraw, in an interview in Pittsburg:

> Ban Johnson has not been on the level with me per-sonally. . . . I introduced Ban Johnson to the East. I was his friend. I made him acquainted with those who are now his intimate acquaintances in the East. I played him square and did not know that he was the man to frame things up. . . . The method he used to queer me, and just at a time when the Baltimore Club was beginning to play, was to suspend me indefi-nitely and otherwise persecute me by jobs that he framed up with his umpires. . . . Now after Johnson caused me to lose $3,900 of my own hard-earned money, I have the whip-hand.

Johnson's response was that "McGraw's statements are ridiculous" and that "it is not what McGraw says. Mr. Brush controls the situation, and he is dictating to McGraw. President Herrmann, of the Cincinnati club, told me once that Mr. Brush was afraid to play an American League club, and now I am sure of it."

However, it was still late July and there were more than two months to go before the 1904 season was over and the World Series could start. There was ample time for changes of minds and plans, and no one was panicking at this point.

The first club the Highlanders met on their early August road trip was Detroit, in Bennett Park. After dropping the first game, the New Yorkers came storming back to take the next three. Griffith's team had caught fire at the same time the Pilgrims and White Sox were slumping, and this happy combination moved the Highlanders, on August 5, for the first time in their two-year existence, into first place on the basis of percentage points. From here, it was logical to project the New York American League club into the World Series picture, a prospect that, no doubt, tied the stomachs of John Brush and John McGraw into tight knots. The "Invaders," as National League rooters often called them, had a shot at the World Championship—in their second season in the big leagues. It had been fifteen years since the Giants could be called champions of anything, and now they might be eclipsed by the Highlanders. All the glory the Giants had worked so hard to attain, since McGraw had come to New York in 1902, could be redirected thanks to Elberfeld's sticky glove, Keeler's seeing-eye ground balls, and Chesbro's elusive spitter. It really could happen!

McGraw's winning-at-all-costs philosophy couldn't tolerate the notion of being second best in anything, least of all in the esteem of his team's hometown baseball enthusiasts. So, despite the fact that the Giants went into August with a 9-game lead over the Colts, he looked to improve his club offensively. Mike Donlin, hitter and discipline problem extraordinaire, had been fined and suspended several times in 1904 for breaking team rules and abusing Cincinnati manager Joe Kelley. The Reds made it known that "Turkey Mike"—called that because of his arrogant, strutting manner—was available. *Sporting Life* commented that "Mike Donlin will be in a bad way if no National League club takes him . . . as the American League is closed to him." Ban Johnson couldn't put up with his notorious behavior on and off the field. John McGraw could—or, at least, he thought he could—direct it to the benefit of the Giants' run production.

McGraw had already managed him in Baltimore in 1901, where he hit .341 and stole 33 bases. There was no reason to believe he couldn't do it again successfully in New York. "WHERE HE BELONGS" was the headline of Timothy Sharp's *Sporting News* article on the Giants' acquisition of the man who missed most of the 1902 season while serving a prison sentence for drunken assault. "That old saying of 'birds of a feather flocking together,' " wrote Sharp,

> is beautifully exemplified in the Donlin-McGraw-Brush coalition. This Donlin is a great ball player beyond all question, but in the face of his lurid career, there can be no doubt that the national pastime would be considerably improved by his elimination from it. . . . Every National League club except New York waived claim to him, and President Pulliam wrote a special communication to all the National League executives calling upon them to keep their hands off this man, as he was a disgrace to baseball and it would bring the great game into disrepute to longer countenance him and his methods. . . .
>
> There was the rowdy Mike Donlin temporarily on the shelf and six magnates pulling to keep him there; but he isn't worried, for he knows he has a friend in that prince of rowdies the only Muggsy, and Brush has always stood by him.

As compensation for Donlin, the Giants sent rookie outfielder Harry "Moose" McCormick to Cincinnati, where he was immediately transferred to Pittsburg for outfielder Jimmy Sebring. Statistically, the Giants really made out well: Donlin was hitting .356 in 60 games, McCormick .266 in 59 games, and Sebring .269 in 80 games. The great question was whether Donlin was going to give New York's pennant objective his full attention.

Donlin was and always had been a star with the bat. There were also a number of stars with the bat and glove—

Napoleon Lajoie, for example. And there were a few stars with the bat, glove, and speed—Willie Keeler, for another example. But the fellow who came to town with the third-place Pittsburg Pirates to play the Giants in mid-August was the best of them all in his day and, perhaps, ever. His given name was Johannes Peter Wagner, but players, fans, and writers called him "Honus," "Hans," or "the Flying Dutchman." He was one of nine children born to Bavarian immigrants who settled in Mansfield (now Carnegie), Pennsylvania. Coal mining was how people earned their living in Mansfield, and that is what "Honus's" father did—and what "Honus" did until he began playing baseball. In 1895, he was plucked from the obscurity of the Iron-Oil League by Ed Barrow, future manager of the Tigers and Red Sox and future business manager of the Yankees through the 1920s, '30s, and early '40s. "There is no doubt about Hans Wagner topping them all," said Barrow. "So uniformly good was Wagner as a player that it is almost impossible to determine whether his highest point of superiority was in his fielding, in his batting average or in his base running. He was a topnotcher in all." John McGraw agreed, calling Wagner "the perfect player." Sam Crawford, an opponent while in the National League with the Cincinnati Reds, also stated flat-out that "the greatest all-around player who ever lived was Honus Wagner." He

> could play any position. He could do everything. In fact, when I first played against him he was an outfielder, and then he became a third baseman, and later the greatest shortstop of them all. Honus could play any position except pitcher and be easily the best in the league at it. He was a wonderful fellow, terrific arm, very quick, all over the place grabbing sure hits and turning them into outs. . . .
>
> You'd never think of it to look at him, of course. He looked so awkward, bowlegged, barrel-chested,

about 200 pounds, a big man. And yet he could run like a scared rabbit. He had enormous hands, and when he scooped up the ball at shortstop he'd grab half the infield with it. But boy, Honus made those plays! He looked awkward doing it, not graceful like Larry Lajoie, but he could make every play Lajoie could make and more.

As a hitter, Honus was a terror. A right-hander who stood deep in the box and far off the plate, he would turn his bat in a little circle until the pitcher released the ball. Then he would stride forward and slash line drives to all fields. "Wagner had no weakness at the plate," wrote Joseph Reichler, "unless it was a base on balls. It was practically impossible to walk him. He'd even chase a waste pitch." In fact, as Reichler points out, the batter's box was given official numerical definition because of Wagner's roaming all around the home plate area. He led the National League in batting average eight times; in hits, two times; in doubles, eight times; in triples, three times; in RBIs, four times; in runs scored, two times; and in stolen bases, five times. Furthermore, he was, as *New York Times* reporter John Kiernan phrased it, a "model of deportment. He never gave his manager any trouble. He was steady and reliable, day in and day out. He had all the solid virtues."

What was it, then, that led to the greatest player with the most even temperament being thrown out of the Giant-Pirate game on August 17? The specific situation, according to Wagner, was his objection to McGraw's interference with a throw from Pirate third baseman Tommy Leach. More important was the greater context: the total frustration on the part of Wagner and the rest of the Pirates at the ever greater likelihood that their three-year reign as National League champs was going to end in 1904 at the hands of the full-throttle New York Giants. The New Yorkers' trip to Pittsburg in mid-July gave serious evidence of this. The local press raised its lance against the first-place Giants. "No National League baseball team that has appeared this season has shown so rowdy a spirit as that exhibited by the Giants on the present trip," said one writer. "The buzzing of the pennant bee about their ears has probably turned the heads of most of the metropolitans, and they are as stuck up as a country beau out with his best girl." The hard feelings carried over into 1905. McGraw complained that he and his team could not go into Pittsburg

> without having some kind of run-in with the fans. . . . We used to suit up at the old Monongahela Hotel and drive to the game in open carriages. Exposition Park was then in Allegheny City, across the river. To reach the bridge, we had to pass a public market. . . . One day we had to dodge handfuls of gravel, loose pieces of brick, and anything throwable all the way to the bridge.

But it wasn't only the kranks in Pittsburg who resented the turn in the Giants' fortune in 1904. Chicagoans, who probably felt an urban rivalry with New York in a general way, were brought to a fever pitch by the Colts' vain effort, thus far, to catch the McGravians. During the second game of a rain-forced Friday double-header on August 24, with the Colts' having already lost a 3-hitter to Christy Mathewson, 3–0, West Side Grounds spectators began throwing soda and beer bottles onto the field. Right fielder George Browne was hit on the leg and narrowly escaped being struck in the back of the head as he was about to haul in a fly ball. As Browne and the other outfielders began to remove some of the glass around them, McGraw dashed at umpire "Blind Bob" Emslie, as the Giant manager usually referred to him, and told him that his team would not continue the game until the field was cleared. By the time order was restored, it was too dark to continue.

Of course, the McGraw-led Giants could get rowdy, too, from time to time. In late August, they concluded their long road trip with a two-day stop in Cincinnati. Redland Field, built in 1902, was called the "Palace of the Fans." It was modeled on the architecture exhibited at the Chicago World's Fair of 1893, the "Columbian Exposition," complete with ornate pillars and columns. "It was far from a practical building from a moneymaking standpoint," writes Ritter Collett, "but it fitted ideally the relaxed atmosphere of old Zinzinnati." Running a very short distance from both first- and third-base foul lines was "Rooters' Row," a forerunner of today's box seats. There waiters sold beer in mugs at twelve for a dollar. This cascade of beer and the extremely close proximity of the stands to the field led to easy and frequent exchanges between spectators and players. In the first of the Giants-Reds three-game set, on Thursday, August 30, the Giants got 3 runs in an eighth-inning rally and snatched away a 3–1 victory for Mathewson. The next day, the two teams would end the month with a double-header. The umpire who was to work both ends, alone, was the "Chief," Charley Zimmer. Zimmer insisted he liked umpiring better than playing. But Zimmer had not anticipated the events he would be part of on August 31. The *New York Herald* declared that an account of the first game would have to read more like a report back from the Russo-Japanese war front than the narration of peaceful baseball: "There were attacks, en masse, on the flank, in the center; there were sorties, skirmishes, assaults and sieges." Joe McGinnity and Jack Harper were the pitchers. The former carried a 28–7 record into the contest, and the latter was on his way to a 23–9 season and held a 2–0 mark against the Giants. "When artillerists of their capacity are up, it increases the tension," observed the *New York Herald*. Both sides were on Zimmer from the outset and would not let up. Finally, Zimmer had it and McGann and Dahlen were thrown out for arguing a safe call on a Cincinnati steal of second base. "You would have thought the crime of the century would have been pulled on Mr. McGann, Dahlen, et al.," said the *Herald*. But all this constituted the preliminary bout before the sixth-inning main event. It was then that foul-tempered catcher Frank Bowerman, who was not in the line-up, left the bench, walked over to "Rooters' Row," and punched a man who had been razzing the Giants for most of the game. At first, the private ballpark police took hold of Bowerman and began to escort him from the field, but Zimmer, the old ballplayer, ordered them to allow him to return to the New York bench. The man who had been punched and had his jaw cut, Albert Hartzell, a music teacher and son of a member of the Cincinnati Board of Education, appealed to the regular police. "Eight officers came on the field," explained *The New York Times*, "and amid great excitement, took Bowerman in custody." At this time, the Giant players began to move on the police in an apparent effort to rescue Bowerman; however, they ultimately decided to back down and off went their teammate under arrest. First, Hartzell claimed that McGraw ordered the assault, laying grounds for a juicy lawsuit; but, for whatever reason—perhaps unfavorable family publicity—he reconsidered the matter and decided not to prosecute at all. Regarding the games themselves, the Giants swept the double-header, 3-2 in eleven innings and 4–1 in a seven–inning game shortened so that the visitors could catch a train home to New York. The Giants had posted a 22–8 record for August, 84–32 overall, and went into September with a 15-game lead over the second-place Colts.

Temper tantrums born of the nerves that hard competitors cannot always control in a pennant race were not confined to the National League. In an early August series between the Highlanders and Blues, held in Cleveland, a number of the New Yorkers battled with umpire Frank H. "Silk" O'Loughlin. O'Loughlin was an extremely popular umpire with the fans. Of all his antics, they especially loved his distinctive call "Str-r-ike Tuh!" "Kids used to be taken to the game and admonished to listen for this cry," writes Robert Smith. "When he gave it, just as odd and abrupt as it had been described, the young fans would yell in delight." But his broad flourishes were not always appreciated by the players. "Silk" was supposed to have worn a diamond ring which sparkled brightly in the sun. Eugene Murdock asserts that "players accused him of calling runners out more than safe simply to flash his 'cracked ice.'" Another reason players did not care for him was his short fuse. "More than once after a howling player would tell him how blind he was," states James Kahn, "he would listen for a while and then swing his arm up in banishment and proclaim: 'Get out of here. I never missed one in my life. Too late to start now. The Pope for religion. O'Loughlin for baseball. Both infallible.'" In the fourth inning of the game on August 8, with the Blues ahead, 7–1, Dave Fultz and John Ganzel objected to O'Loughlin's strike calls. When Fultz and manager Griffith continued to complain, they were ordered to their bench. When they refused, O'Loughlin called for a police officer and the two were led off the field. The next day Jack Powell, knocked out of the box in the fourth inning, blamed O'Loughlin for his problem and was bounced. Later, Jimmy Williams followed him, with a police escort. When Griffith and Williams received suspensions for their behavior, Highlander owner Frank Farrell vowed that O'Loughlin would, under no circumstances, be allowed to enter Hilltop Park. However, when, at the end of the month, Cleveland visited New York, O'Loughlin marched through the gates and assumed his scheduled position behind the plate. "I let O'Loughlin into the grounds," Farrell told reporters, "because I must comply with the constitution and rules of the American League." Ban Johnson was in charge of this circuit.

It was in early September that the pitching ace of the

Highlanders, Jack Chesbro, won his 30th game of the season. The standings on that day had New York atop the American League by a half-game over Boston. Championship fever had invaded Hilltop Park as well as the Polo Grounds. A crowd of 24,632 Highlander fans headed for Washington Heights to see Griffith's high-geared club take on the third-place Athletics in a Labor Day double-header. Traditionally, it was at this event that—win, lose, or draw—men would enjoy marking the coming of fall by sailing their summer straw hats onto the field. Today, in the first game, they got the added enjoyment of seeing Chesbro, with a single day's rest, win again by a 2–1 score. Through seven innings, the New York pitching machine had a 1-hitter. In the eighth, he faltered a bit, giving up 3 hits and a run. But, recharged, he set the A's down in the ninth and earned yet another "W." Although Jack Powell lost the second game, the Highlanders won both contests the next day—back-to-back double-headers—and maintained their half-game lead.

As much as they won, it seemed impossible for the Highlanders to gain a comfortable lead over the second-place Pilgrims. When a pennant-contending club makes a deal, the hope is to add that one player who will pick things up a notch—and one notch's distance is what the Highlanders needed badly as the season went into its final stretch. Virgil "Ned" Garvin, a 6-foot-3½ Texan in his sixth year, had won 15 games in 1903 with the Superbas. He had gotten effective use out of that same screwball that served Christy Mathewson so well. But why would seventh-place Brooklyn, hardly able to field a truly major league level team, release him? The answer was that for all of Garvin's promise, he had a touch of "Turkey Mike" Donlin in him and Ned Hanlon had had enough. In early May, Garvin was suspended for having spent the previous evening in a Philadelphia saloon, outside of which he was badly injured in a mugging by his drinking companions. Just recently, on a train ride from St. Louis to

Cincinnati, he got drunk, beat up club secretary George Watson, and smashed the windows of the Pullman sleeper. "What he can do as a pitcher," commented John B. Foster in *Sporting Life,*

> isn't worth talking about. He might be one of the best men who ever walked into the pitcher's box, but he doesn't seem to know it, and so long as he doesn't seem to know it, perhaps it isn't worthwhile trying to tell him about it. There is an idea in Brooklyn, and I don't think it is far out of the way, that Garvin has done quite a lot all the year to upset the team. Not with intent, but simply because it is his disposition. He did the same thing with Chicago.

This is exactly the element that Ban Johnson, from the first, discouraged in the American League. Yet, even with all that was known of Garvin's littered past and unmanageable character, Johnson still allowed the Highlanders to sign the wayward pitcher to a player's contract. This, as much as anything else during the 1904 season, indicated what a strong New York team meant to the American League president.

On Wednesday, September 7, "Hooks" Wiltse recorded his 10th straight win for the Giants, still having no experience with defeat in the big leagues. This was a very professional, 6–3 performance, in which he spaced 8 Phillie hits. It occurred in the opener of a seven–game series at the Polo Grounds. Such lengthy meetings late in the season were made necessary by earlier rain outs and games called on account of darkness. To squeeze in all seven contests, double-headers were scheduled for the next three days. In the first game, on September 8, Luther Taylor (18–11) lost 9–8 to the Phillies' "Frosty Bill" Duggleby. In the second, "Matty," for the second year in a row, won his 30th. This late affair, which lasted six and a half innings, shortened by darkness, was interesting because it showed the kind of balanced offense the Giants benefited from all year long. Although they scored only 4 runs to the Phillies' 1, their 10 hits, off Tom "Tully" Sparks, came from all nine players.

The games on September 9, attended by 1,844 very uncomfortable people, were played in weather forecasting the change of seasons. "A cold north wind painted every nose blue," wrote the *New York Herald* reporter. "Ten thousand empty seats were just so many Aeolian harps for the wind to blow upon and nobody cared particularly whether the visitors won or lost." McGinnity gave up 12 hits but won his 31st—his second year in a row over 30. The second game was called after five innings with darkness setting in before either team could cross the plate. The *Herald* called the play in this shortened contest "automaton baseball": "Nobody wanted to do anything and most of them could not have done it if they had tried. Leon Ames went in to keep warm for New York, while the sometime smiling [Frank] Corridon went against him. He didn't smile yesterday. He was afraid his face might freeze that way." While the weather eased up a bit the next afternoon, the Phillies did not, forcing the home team into two 1-run ball games. A Saturday crowd of 15,250 got to see their favorites score 2 in the ninth on a Bresnahan triple to win the first game, 5–4. Wiltse pitched this one, winning his 11th straight, still without a loss. For most of the second game, Luther Taylor had things in hand. Going into the ninth, the score stood 6–3 and the Phillies had not made any offensive noise in four innings. Then two singles, an error, and a ground ball pulled the visitors within 1 run. However, the rally ended there and so did the seven-game series. The New Yorkers had their double victory for the day and a 5–1–1 record for the grueling four afternoons' work. This made for an overall account of 93–33. Closest to them were the Colts, 76–50, and the Pirates, 73–50. This meant that Chicago trailed by 17 games and Pittsburg by 18-1/2. Both the Giants and the Colts had 28 games left, which made the magic number 12. Any combination of 12 New York wins and Chicago losses would send the pennant to the Polo Grounds. According to *Sporting Life*, the Giant players balked at their owner's plan for a world tour with the Colts. But now it reported that Brush was organizing a trip to Cuba. "All those who are going," the weekly journal was told, "have already deposited $100 each as a guarantee that they will make the tour."

Just as the Giants and Phillies had been forced by prior postponements into three consecutive double-headers at the Polo Grounds, the Highlanders and Pilgrims faced the same ordeal at the Huntington Avenue Grounds in Boston. The difference, however, was considerable. The former could change very little in the fortunes of the clubs involved; the latter could change everything. As of the morning of September 14, the day the first of the two-game sets was to be played, the Pilgrims held a half-game lead over the Highlanders. Six games divided in a lopsided way meant first place. Pitching for Boston in the opener was "Big Bill" Dinneen, on his way to a third straight 20-win season. His opposite number, with a day's rest between starts, was Jack Chesbro. Despite awful weather, 8,515 fans crowded the small grandstand and bleachers. Rain had been falling all morning and continued when the game began; and a thick fog hung over the field, making it difficult to see. But visibility did not seem to be a problem for Patsy Dougherty, who, after receiving a warm greeting from his former hometown fans, lined a single to right to start the game. Keeler followed with a bunt down the third base line that catcher Lou Criger picked up and heaved all the way to the bleachers. Dougherty did not stop circling the bases until he scored the series' first run. Elberfeld then sacrificed Keeler to third, from which he scored New York's second run on a high bounder off the bat of Williams that even slick fielding

Boston third baseman and manager Jimmy Collins couldn't grab. Two innings later, Keeler bunted successfully for the second time, was again advanced by an Elberfeld sacrifice, went to third on an error by shortstop Freddy Parent, and scored on Williams' fly to center. Boston's only tally came in the last of the ninth, when Collins' single to left got by Dougherty for a 2-base error, and a wild pitch by Chesbro—probably an errant spitter—allowed the Pilgrim leader to complete the circuit. Norwood Gibson and Jack Powell threw in the second game, which, because of darkness, lasted only five innings with the score locked at 1–1. But the day had been good for the New Yorkers. "Manager Clark Griffith and his Greater New York team lead for the American League championship," boasted *The New York Times*, "and Griffith says he will hold the lead until the end." The Highlander field boss spoke too soon. Boston outscored New York 3–2 in Thursday's early game and reclaimed the league's top spot. Jesse Tannehill, having a fine year in Boston after his mediocre one in New York in 1903, kept the 9 hits he surrendered to his old teammates relatively innocuous and got the win over Al Orth. Once more, the second half of the double-header ended in a 1–1 tie, this time after a full nine innings. George "Sassafras" Winter and Jack Powell were responsible for this well-pitched but inconclusive contest.

More than 16,000 had attended Thursday's battles and almost 23,000, reputed to be the largest crowd in Boston's baseball history, inched their way in for Friday's series-ending double-header. It was to be another Dinneen-Chesbro match-up in the opener. The visitors made their mark immediately with 3 runs in the first and 3 more in the second. Dinneen then settled down while his club fought back with 1 in the fifth and 3 in the seventh. But Chesbro made the 6–4 lead stand up for the balance of the game, and he had his 7th consecutive victory, to bring his personal numbers to 35–8 and move his team into first place for the second time in three days. After a short break, Boston sent "Cy" Young out against "Ned" Garvin to try to recapture the half-game edge that kept slipping away from both teams. The Pilgrims seemed to like the deliveries of the ex-Superba, as they scored twice in the second and once in the third, forcing Griffith to bring in Ambrose Puttman, the young lefty. "Farmer" Young gave up runs himself in the fifth and ninth, but he had the Highlanders well enough in hand to chalk up a 4–2 triumph. So, in the six games played, each team won twice and lost twice, and there were 2 ties to underscore the quality and equality of play in this extremely exciting series. If they both kept their records intact through the rest of September and October, there would be a spectacular show-down awaiting them at the very end of the season, when they were scheduled to meet on the Hilltop in New York.

The Giants, meanwhile, moved inexorably toward their championship. By September 21, the magic number was one. Already, the management let the players begin to enjoy the fruits of their labor, accepting an invitation from The Four-teenth Street Theatre to attend the musical comedy "Girls Will Be Girls," with Al Leach and The Three Rosebuds. Further, the Giant organization announced its intention to stage a "Field Day" on October 6 at the Polo Grounds. The program would include, said *The New York Times*, "a baseball game between the coming champions and a picked team, ball throwing contests, running the bases, and boxing exhibi-tions between men of national reputation." Sometimes, un-happily, a letdown in performance is the price paid for adula-tion and self-indulgence, and there was a hint that the Giants might be undergoing such a phenomenon in their late Sep-tember series with Cincinnati.

In the first game of a double-header, on Wednesday, September 21, the New Yorkers, playing at home before 9,000 rooters hoping to witness their team's 100th victory and pennant clincher, lost a 6–4 decision. The defeated Giant pitcher was Christy Mathewson, whose record was now 31–11. The sizable mid-week crowd sat tight, expecting that the second game would definitely provide the National League banner. Instead, it saw McGraw's men held scoreless by Jack Harper and lose, 2–0. Not only was this the third time Harper had beaten New York this year, with only 1 loss, but this was the first time New York had lost three times in a row since 1903. Obviously, there was no serious reason for alarm. So far from troubled was McGraw that he decided to make the next game against Cincinnati a historic occasion in two ways. This would be the one that made his club's National League championship official, and it would occur with a Giant catcher, "Orator Jim" O'Rourke, who would be playing in his fourth decade of major league ball. O'Rourke was one of the most appreciated players and personalities in National League history. He began playing the game back in 1866 in his hometown and permanent residence of Bridgeport, Connecticut. After four fine years in the National Association of Professional Base Ball Players, the first professional major league, O'Rourke moved into the National League with the Boston Red Stockings. In this new circuit's first game, Boston *v.* Philadelphia, O'Rourke was the third batter. When he lined a single to left, he recorded the National League's first official hit ever. So many hits followed from O'Rourke's bat that when, in 1879, he decided to play for the Providence Grays because of a dispute over who should pay for his uniform, owner Arthur H. Soden decided to draw up baseball's first reserve clause for his Boston players' contracts. By 1885, O'Rourke was in New York, playing the outfield, occasionally catching, and hitting at a .300 clip for the Giants. There he remained for seven years. In 1888 and 1889, he was the left fielder for the only two Giant pennant winners to date. When his eighteen-year playing career was over, O'Rourke, a proud, intelligent, and garrulous man—hence "Orator Jim"—practiced law, farmed, and used his baseball skills to organize, manage, and play in the Connecticut League. In 1900, at the age of forty-eight, he hit .358, and so, was in reasonably good shape and form when McGraw asked him to step behind the plate to make the connection between the team on the verge of gaining the 1904 banner and the previous champion clubs of '88 and '89.

Only 4,200 were in the ballpark for the double-header on Thursday, September 22. Although the afternoon was chillier than usual, the most likely explanation for the relatively poor turnout was the justified conviction that the single victory needed to ice first place would come today, tomorrow, or the next day, so what was the point in running oneself ragged at this moment? In the first game, McGinnity took the mound for New York, opposed by southpaw Winford "Win" Kellum. Although the Reds opened the scoring in the top of the second with 1 run, the home club answered immediately with 3 and then got 4 more in the fourth. While Cincinnati did make a run at New York in the late stages of the game, bringing the score to 7–5, the gap was narrowed no further and the Giants donned their well-deserved National League crown. O'Rourke caught all nine innings and went 1 for 4. "Orator Jim's" past glories occupied the catching box at the instant of victory, but the greatest share of the credit was due the strong man on the rubber, Joe McGinnity, whose record for the current season rose to 34–7. Following the game, the sale of seats took place for a Giant players' benefit at Klaw and Erlanger's New York Theater, on Broadway at Forty-fifth Street, to be held during the evening of October 2. Grateful fans with money in their pockets would bid on theater boxes, the proceeds going to the players as a bonus for their much appreciated work in bringing New York top honors in the National League.

For the Giants, with the pennant already in hand, the rest of the season did not appear to mean much. In fact, judging from the way they played on September 23, it did not appear to mean anything at all. "Red" Ames was given the start by McGraw, and although he gave up only 3 runs to the potent Pirate hitters, he was less than impressive. In the ninth, trailing 3–0, McGraw replaced Ames with catcher Frank Bowerman. The explanation, as *The New York Times* had it, was that "it was the best change that could have been made under the circumstances, for it was said, there was no other pitcher on the grounds." "Niagara Frank" gave up 4 runs in the only inning he ever pitched in the big leagues, and the Giants fell behind and lost by a score of 7–0. "PITTSBURG PLAYS ALL BY ITSELF," read the headline in the *New York Herald:*

> You had to explain to chance visitors yesterday that the team had played differently earlier in the year and had not received the pennant at a donation or found it in a job lot of trading stamps. Some of the chance visitors were even skeptical when told of this and said that, having come from Missouri, they would have to have a physical demonstration. There is no telling what they think, for it was impossible to show them. . . . "If they don't want to play ball, let them close the Polo Grounds," was a general comment. "The criminal code ought to have a section in it about obtaining money for an exhibition of that kind."

The next day, properly chastised, the Giants pulled it together and, behind Matthewson's 4-hitter, defeated the third-place Pirates, 3–1. "Matty's" record was now 32–11. During the game, time out was called for Harry Stevens, the "scorecard man." Stevens was an English immigrant iron molder who got sidetracked by a clever commercial concept to which he dedicated himself totally. Blanche McGraw remembered seeing him in Columbus, Ohio, in the early days of his venture:

> [He] was a little man with a bright red coat and cap. . . . He went through the small grandstand yell-

ing in a booming voice how it was impossible to tell which player was which unless you bought one of his hand-printed score sheets for a nickel, with or without a pencil. He also sold his own roasted peanuts. All through the games he waved his cap at fans and even at the players. He was a happy and friendly fellow supporting a wife and five kids in Niles, Ohio, on a simple idea.

Stevens had made a secure place for himself at the Polo Grounds by this time and was doing quite well financially, although absolutely nothing compared to what the Harry M. Stevens operation would do in sports arenas in a later day. The reason for the time out was to give Stevens the opportunity to present John Brush with a large loving cup inscribed with the names of the players "as a token of esteem." A trophy representing the year's fine achievement and mutual esteem obviously meant a great deal to this Giant organization and was a nice touch, but it continued to look to the New York baseball public that the National League champs considered the 1904 season over.

On September 28, in a game against the second-place Colts, it was evident that the team was suffering from a rapid disintegration. Gilbert, Bresnahan, and McGraw, himself, were not even present this afternoon. *The New York Times* called the Giants' play "listless," and the *New York Herald* commented that "about the only satisfaction a goodly number of baseball enthusiasts who paid to see New York and Chicago play at the Polo Grounds yesterday had was to hiss the local team at the conclusion of nine dreary, uninteresting innings." The day after, even "Matty" had joined the boys just playing out the string. To the *Times*, he "seemed to simply toss the ball to the batsmen." In the seventh inning, "Matty" "hit a ball to Tinker, who threw Bowerman out at second, and Evers easily caught Mathewson at first, who loped toward the base with the bat in his hand." Tinker to Evers to Chance—but not challenged by the usual all-out

Giant base running. The *New York World* repeated a remark made by "a bleacherite . . . as he passed slowly through the gates after the game": "Where do they think we get the money?" "Baseball, for the present season," said the *Herald*, "seems to be at an end so far as the Giants are concerned."

But—weren't there any thoughts at all about taking the National League championship and putting it up against the American League championship, the stakes being the greater World Championship? On the evening of September 25, John Brush made the statement that America's baseball fans feared was coming. First Brush congratulated his Giants for "winning the championship of the United States in the National League of Professional Baseball Clubs" and gave special credit to John McGraw, who "as a manager of a baseball club stands alone and is without a rival." He then went on to the point of it all, the sidestepping of the World Series—and this by route of the degradation of the American League:

> One of the purposes of the National League, according to Article 4, Section 2 of the constitution, is to establish and regulate the professional baseball championship of the United States. From the beginning this has been an annual event, and each year after the strenuous work of playing the schedule, the victorious club has rested from its work and has worn its laurels unquestioned until they were won from it in some succeeding year by some other club of the National League. There is nothing in the constitution or playing rules of the National League which requires its victorious club to submit its championship honors to a contest with a victorious club of a minor league.
>
> There may be those who think the winner in the Eastern or in the Southern or some other league is superior to the winner in the National. That is their privilege to so believe and there can be no criticism for such opinions, but that furnishes no reason why the champion of the National should enter into a contest with them.

The club that won from the clubs that represent the cities of Boston, Brooklyn, New York, Philadelphia, Pittsburg, Cincinnati, Chicago and St. Louis—the eight largest and most important cities in America—in a series of 154 games, is entitled to the honor of champions of the United States, without being called upon to contend with or recognize clubs from minor league towns.

The reaction on the part of the public and press was instantaneous and overwhelmingly vigorous in its criticism of Brush's argument and his action. First of all, Brush's sense of history was warped, as *The New York Times, Sporting Life,* and others pointed out. National League pennant winners had played a World Series against American Association pennant winners every year from 1884 through 1890. Then, when the American Association folded, the National League held a split season, in 1892, after which the two half-season winners played a World Series to determine an overall champion. From 1894 through 1897, while the National League operated a twelve-team monopoly, the first two teams played the Temple Cup Series, a similar postseason challenge. In 1900, without the incentive of Colonel William C. Temple's trophy, the National league felt obliged to schedule a World Series and style it after the Temple Cup play-off. And, finally, in 1903, when the National League and American League made peace, the Pittsburg Pirates of the "senior circuit" did not hesitate to challenge the Boston Pilgrims of the "junior circuit" to the first World Series in the modern major league arrangement. The World Series was not some new crackbrained idea. By 1904 it had a long and storied past. There was the total dominance of Charley "Old Hoss" Radbourne of the Providence Grays over the New York Metropolitans (Mets) in the first World Series in 1884; Curt Welch's $15,000 slide to score the run that gave the St. Louis Browns their triumph over the Chicago White Stockings in 1886; "Sir

Timothy" Keefe's day-in-day-out pitching heroics in the New York Giants' crushing of the St. Louis Browns in 1888; the bruising 1895 Temple Cup match-up of the Baltimore Orioles and Cleveland Spiders, probably the two most physical teams ever on the same field; and Bill Dinneen's 2 shutouts thrown in 3 victories for the Boston Pilgrims in the previous year's (1903) World Series—among a host of other memories that various people kept with warm feelings and exchanged with hometown pride.

Regarding a preseason decision on the subject of a World Series in 1904, Ban Johnson asserted that the Joint Schedule Committee, meeting in New York, "resolved that the champions of both leagues this fall should play off the world's championship." However, Jim Hart rejected this account, explaining that the agreement was "only verbal in committee. The National League as a body never acted on the measure and no such important action could be decided upon without a vote of the various presidents."

Speaking for the neglected fans, *The New York Times* declared that Brush's course of action

> will undoubtedly be a disappointment to nine-tenths of the people who patronize the game in this city, and is likely to have an injurious effect on the future popularity of the New York [Giant] Club. If the Greater New York, Boston, or any other club should win the American League championship, not one of the reasons set forth in Mr. Brush's statement, from a sportsman's point of view, would hold good if the Polo Grounds representatives refused to play the new champions of the American League.

It dismissed Brush's classification of the American League as a minor league as "poor judgment": "With the pick of the National League Players in its ranks, and with a powerful circuit of cities, the American League is rated by baseball critics throughout the country as equal, if not stronger, in playing strength to the older organization." The *New York World*, assuming a New York victory in the American League, stated that

> public demand for the usual series of games between the Giants and the Highlanders, local clubs in the National and American Leagues respectively, which will decide the world's championship, will not be satisfied with the assertion of President Brush that the Giants are willing to close the season satisfied with National honors.
>
> It is even uncertain if the neatly typewritten statement of Mr. Brush strengthens his position in declining the post-season schedule, since the "fans" will fail to find any good reason why he should set aside all precedent through the discovery he has made in reading Article 4, Section 2, of the National Constitution.

"What right has John T. Brush," a man "well posted on baseball affairs" said to the *New York World*,

> to deprive the baseball public of an opportunity to see what would undoubtedly be the most interesting baseball series ever played? He gets his money from the sport-loving public of this city and should consider their wishes. The document sent out by Brush, giving his alleged reasons for not going after the world's championship, is the weakest statement of the kind I ever read or heard. In the first place Brush's hidden slur placing the American League in the minor league class is so stupid it will not even deceive the bat boys at the Polo Grounds, to say nothing of any grown person that follows the game.

The *New York Herald* printed a letter from C. Allyn Stephens, a fan who called Brush's statement "inane" and wondered,

> Is it possible that Mr. Brush underestimates the effect of his present position in refusing to play a series of

post season games? Does he not realize the potent effect of declining to compete for the world's championship? Will the paying public continue to patronize a league that practically confesses to being afraid to attain the greatest honor? Is it fair to those players who have done so splendidly throughout the season and now wish for the attainment of the greatest honor?

Public opinion says play! and few there are who have dared to face public opinion and attempt its overthrow!

Timothy Sharp, in *The Sporting News,* saw Brush's position on the World Series as "so internally selfish that it chills the blood of every true sportsman." "The great American public," Sharp contended, in images and phrases designed to pierce the Brush smugness,

likes a game sportsman and if Mr. Brush were of the true make-up, instead of the fish-blood and bag-of-bones variety, he would proclaim that he was sure he had the best club and would back his aggregation for money or marbles against any outfit that could be gotten together. . . . He may say he is not afraid of the outcome, but his acts give the lie to such an assertion. To sum it up briefly, if he were absolutely sure that his club would win, no man on Earth believes he would decline an encounter for an instant.

That is a plain act of cowardice and no sophistry can palliate that offense in the public eye. There is a good chance that the Giants might be licked. Here you have the Alpha and Omega of the whole business. . . . Taking care of Number One has always been John T. Brush's hobby. . . .

And the *Chicago Sunday Tribune* struck at the same target, the Giant management's fear of losing, adding to it a touch of strongly brewed anti-New York spirit:

If Brush thought he had a team which could beat the American League champions he would welcome such a series, because it would enhance his prestige. If he was any kind of sportsman he would play the series if he expected to get licked, rather than face the charges of quitting. But Brush does not think the Giants can win. He is a shrewd observer of men and things, and realizes fully the strength of his rivals. He is a businessman, and not in any sense of the word a sportsman.

Knowing the New York public as well as he does, he knows what would happen if the Giants played the American League champions and lost. . . . Brush is taking desperate chances, therefore, to retain the hold the Giants have there and prevent any possible shattering of his public idols.

Highlander manager Clark Griffith, who had earlier gone on record as hoping for a Giant pennant and a Giant-Highlander World Series, spewed out his utter contempt for the Giant management:

Brush's statement is not a surprise to us. He always was a sure thing fellow, and his remarks show that he is hiding behind a bush. McGraw was in the American League and he knows what he is up against when he tackles an American League team. . . .

McGraw knows well that almost any team in the American League can beat the Giants, so it is no wonder to me that he is fighting shy of a series with the Yankees. It's no wonder Muggsy is afraid to play. He hasn't a hitter in his infield and our outfield has got his beat a block. That team of his has been up against a lot of easy marks all summer—teams that Washington could put it all over—and his men have won the pennant, not because they can play ball, but because the other fellows can't.

Griffith's use of the nickname "Muggsy" was calculated to enrage McGraw. He got it in Baltimore as a result of a resemblance to a local politician, a comic strip, or both. In any case, he hated it enormously. "It acted on him like a red flag waved in front of a bull," asserted Fred Lieb, "and no oath or vulgarity got under his skin as much as the hated 'Muggsy.' "

McGraw, for the moment, was silent. But some of his players were not. According to journalist Sam Crane, one of them claimed that he and his teammates wanted to play the World Series for the money:

> We have decided to take the matter in our hands and we will complete all arrangements the instant it is known which club is to win the American League pennant.
> There will be a barrel of money in it for us, whichever club wins, and we are not going to allow any personal differences Brush and McGraw may have with Ban Johnson to stop us from getting the money. We will have lived up to our contracts with the New York Club on October 15, and will then be free to play whom we like.
> I don't see where the club would have any kick coming on that. We have done our share this year, you can bet your life. The club will make more money than ever before in the history of the game, and I don't think we are looking for too much by wanting to get what we can from the series. And I want to tell you that the Giants feel sure that they can beat the American League winners. They will have their money up, too.

This last factor, betting by players and others—**scandal**—worried *Sporting Life*:

> It is to be hoped for the good of the sport that the New York Club will bow to public demand and thus forestall independent action by the players. In the latter event the rival clubs would not only lose a considerable amount of easily earned gate money, but would deprive the contests of the dignity and pres-

tige of league sanction, thus making them mere exhibition games and perhaps pave the way, in the absence of wholesome club restraint, for possible abuses or even scandals.

There is too much of the reputation and prestige of major league ball, irrespective of the mere winning of this series, at stake to permit the rival players to run the show alone, and for this reason, more than all others combined, we think the New York National Club should smother resentment, sacrifice personal feeling, and lend its official countenance to the series.

Here was the greatest danger: the loss of major league baseball's credibility. And, in *The Sporting News,* under the headline "SOURCE OF DANGER," H. G. Merrill gave this problem a name: "John Turmoil Brush." It was time, he submitted, to discard Brush: "Men of the temperament and characteristics of this man have no business in a sport conducted for the entertainment of the American public simply because it is only nature emphasizing itself for them to run counter to public sentiment." What he was doing earned such hostility that fans and journalists fumed in a current of rage that spilled beyond the limits of articulate expression. People just hated him—and McGraw, because the Giant manager was assumed to be in full support of, if not the inspiration for, his boss's position: risk nothing and stay at the top.

7.

The World Championship

O f the remaining six games on the Giants' schedule in October, five were home against the Cardinals. It was difficult to make a sound judgment regarding which was the pennant winner and which the fifth-place team on the basis of the play in this series. Four times the Cardinals were victorious against the team John Brush said had captured the "championship of the United States." "GIANTS STILL IN DEPRESSING FORM," read the *New York Herald*'s headline. *The New York Times* complained about Mertes' playing center field for the absent Bresnahan, characterizing his fielding as bordering "on the ridiculous." And the *New York Daily Tribune* deplored the fact that "it looked as though the [Giants] put no interest in their work. Calls of 'It's too bad you won the championship!' were frequent, and on days that double-headers were played, many spectators left the grounds after the first game." The Giants' losing streak had reached six games, but this did not cut into the enjoyment of the splashy benefit given them on Sunday, October 2, at Klaw and Erlanger's New York Theater. Jockey

Tod Sloan, a close friend and business partner of McGraw's, served as the master of ceremonies. A large number of celebrities were on hand, some even traveling in from out of town. As a group, the politico-show business set gravitated toward baseball and especially the talented players collected by the infamous and therefore all-the-more-attractive management team of McGraw and Brush (whose second wife Elsie Lombard was herself a former actress). Here was a telling recognition of which performers, relying on the adulation of an audience, held the top spot in New York at the time—an acknowledgement that the baseball field, with its honestly engaging characters and largely unpredictable drama, as well as its sizable crowd of uninhibited cheering and jeering fanatics, had emerged as the greatest show in town. Brush encouraged this following by providing politicians and show business personalities with special free passes such as the one designed by Lambert Brothers, the jeweler, in the form of a penknife with a picture of the Polo Grounds set back into the handle. Sports announcer Joe Humphries presented McGraw with a huge loving cup for the organization as well as personal mementos, which included a watch charm set with sixty-eight diamonds from his stage friends, a set of diamond cuff buttons from Harry Stevens, and, as Blanche McGraw put it, "less brilliant items bestowed with equal pride and affection." The benefit itself brought in an astonishing $25,000, all of which was distributed to very grateful players, many of whom didn't earn very much money in salary.

Fewer than 1,000 turned out the next afternoon, October 4, for the double-header against the Cardinals that would formally end the season. McGinnity pitched and lost the opener, 7–3, winding up with a record of 35–8. His teammates made 5 errors in their half-hearted, go-through-the-motions performance. The second game was a total disaster. The trouble began in the bottom of the first when Dan

McGann, who thought he had hit a home run over the right fielder's head, was called out on an appeal play for not touching first base. McGann and acting manager William "Doc" Marshall cornered umpire Jim Johnstone and argued loudly and abusively enough to be ordered off the field. Three innings later, Dahlen started on Johnstone over a safe call at second, and he also was ejected. This was too much for the Giants, who appeared unwilling to resume their positions, forcing Johnstone to forfeit the game to St. Louis. The 2,000 spectators were so worked up by this time, *The New York Times* declared, that they were making "as much noise as could be made by five times that number." As Johnstone attempted to leave the field, he was rushed by a number of these juiced-up Giant loyalists sitting in the grandstand, and violently shoved. Just after this, a fire broke out in the area of the home team players' bench.

Under the headline "DISGRACEFUL END," W. M. Rankin blasted the Giants in his *Sporting News* column:

> [In] the closing scenes on the Polo Grounds, this city . . . was a mix-up of enthusiasts, umpire, players, police and general dissatisfaction. It was the most disgraceful way for a champion team to end so grand and successful a campaign. . . .
>
> To forfeit the last game of the season was not the proper thing for them to do. Their actions during the past few weeks have not been all they should have been or was expected of them. They have acted entirely too indifferent to the duties they were expected to perform. . . . The public should have had a run for its money. It has supported them in grand style this year and was certainly entitled to better treatment from them.

Rankin was an influential journalist commenting in a periodical regarded as "the bible of baseball." If the religious imagery is appropriate, the eighty-year-old man they called

"Father," Henry Chadwick, had to be considered the game's guardian angel. Chadwick had been the first great promoter of the game, the developer of the box score, the author of numerous manuals and books, and the editor of the indispensable annual *Spalding's Official Base Ball Guide*. The most venerable sportswriter of them all couldn't stand what he had witnessed on October 4. He wrote a letter to *The Sporting News* stating that it was "with pained regret" that he had "to record the closing scene of the last game of the New York team at the Polo Grounds for 1904." That evening a specially arranged performance took place at the Majestic Theater, during which a silver-mounted bat, suitably inscribed, was presented to John McGraw and the Giants. Given the day's events, at least some of those present must have been a little uncomfortable.

As the month of October began, the Highlanders held a .003 first-place lead over the Pilgrims. The continued prospect of winning the American League pennant inspired President Joseph Gordon of the Highlanders to make one last attempt to get John Brush to change his mind about playing a World Series:

> John T. Brush, Esq.
> President New York National League Club
>
> Dear Sir:
>
> In behalf of the Greater New York Baseball Club of the American League, I hereby challenge the New York National League Club to play a series of seven games for the world's championship in the event of the winning of the American League pennant by the Greater New Yorks. In view of a general popular demand in the interest of true sportsmanship, I believe that such a series should be arranged forthwith.
>
> As far as the Greater New York Club is concerned, gate receipts cut an insignificant figure. The New

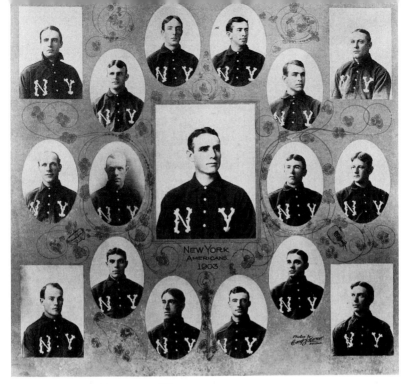

The 1903 New York Highlanders, predecessors of the Yankees, in their very first year in the American League.

The 1904 New York Giants, the National League's most contentious and hated—and best.

John McGraw, "Little Napoleon," the battling old Oriole who managed
and manhandled the Giants to ten pennants in thirty-one years.

Christy Mathewson, Giant pitcher and personality extraordinaire.
"Matty," it was said, "was master of them all."

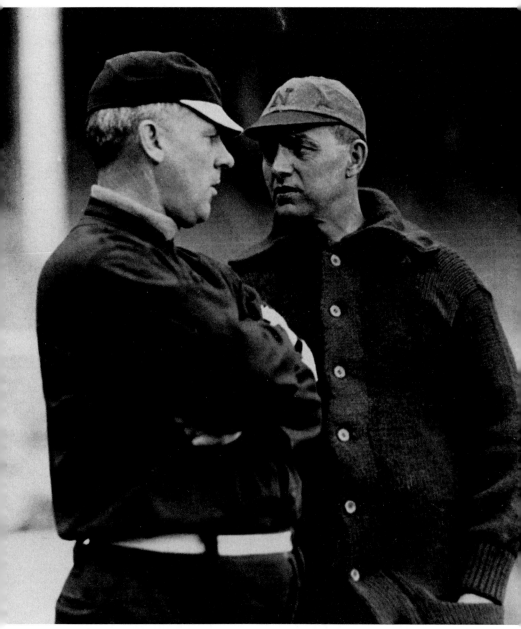

John McGraw and Joe McGinnity, pitching ace of the 1904 Giants. The "Iron Man" could throw all day—and often did.

John T. Brush, the bitter and willful owner of the New York Giants, who saw the American League as a multi-headed emissary from the bowels of hell.

GRIFFITH

Clark Griffith, "the Old Fox," crafty manager-pitcher of the New York Highlanders. Once a players' union radical, he later became the long-time owner of the Washington Senators.

"Wee Willie" Keeler, one of the game's greatest all-around players. Not only could this little Highlander "hit 'em where they ain't," he could catch 'em where they were.

"Happy Jack" Chesbro, burly Highlander spitballer who won a modern
record forty-one games (45 percent of his team's total victories) in 1904.

"Czar" Ban Johnson, president of the American League and baseball's most powerful and provocative figure in the early twentieth century.

An older, demoralized Ban Johnson leaving his Chicago office for the last time after having been forced out of the game.

Harry Pulliam, the other, lesser president (of the National League), whose tormented life was ended tragically by his own hand.

Watching the Giants for free from steep, scrubby Coogan's Bluff behind the grandstand of the Polo Grounds.

The Polo Grounds, Upper Manhattan home of the New York Giants, as seen from behind the overflow crowd allowed to stand in the roped-off deep outfield.

The crowd, properly attired in hats, jackets, and ties, waiting to be admitted to the Polo Grounds. Above and beside these "kranks" (fans) is the
Sixth Avenue "El," the transportation most of the Giants' faithful used to
travel from as far as Wall Street.

American League (better known as "Hilltop") Park, simple and dangerously wooden (possibility of fire!) Upper Manhattan home of the New York Highlanders.

An overflow Hilltop crowd placed shockingly close to the playing field. Obviously, there was little sensitivity to avoiding injury by taking basic precautionary safety measures.

National Baseball Library, Cooperstown, NY.

A game at Hilltop Park with baseball's familiar huge Bull Durham tobacco
advertisement on the distant center-field fence.

The infamous "wild pitch ball" that tormented the Highlanders in the fall of 1904 and Jack Chesbro for the rest of his life.

York public which has supported the game loyally through years of vicissitudes, is entitled to consideration, and the time has now arrived, in my estimation, when this support should be rewarded by the playing of a series that will be memorable in baseball history.

The American League won the title of world's champions when the Bostons defeated the Pittsburgs last year. If the Greater New Yorks defeat the Bostons in the American League race, we will have a right to defend the title. If you wish to prove to the baseball public that the New York Nationals are capable of winning these added laurels from the Greater New Yorks, we will pave the way. The responsibility will rest upon you, Mr. Brush, to accept or decline this fair, square proposition, made in the interests of the national sport.

In stipulating the number of games to be played, we would suggest that three be played at the Polo Grounds, three at American League Park, and the place of the seventh, if it becomes necessary to play it, to be decided by the toss of a coin, the winner of four games to be the champions of the world.

Very truly yours,

Joseph Gordon,
President, Greater New York
Baseball Club of the American
League

When Brush failed to reply to his letter, Gordon told the press that although he had sent his challenge by registered mail, if the Giant owner had not received it, he would be only too willing to mail another one—and, he added, "I think I shall do it." On October 6, Brush responded, giving as the reason for not acting sooner an illness that kept him from his office. He had decided to turn the question over to John McGraw. The Giant manager then issued a statement of his own:

I want to go clearly and emphatically on record in the matter of the refusal of the New York club to play a post-season series. The people of New York have been kind enough to give me some credit for bringing the pennant to New York, and if there is any just blame or criticism for the club's action in protecting that highly-prized honor the blame should rest on my shoulders, not Brush's, for I alone am responsible.

When I came to New York three years ago the team was in last place. Since that time, on and off the field, I have worked to bring the pennant to New York. The result is known. Now that the New York team has won this honor, I for one will not stand to see it tossed away like a rag. The pennant means something to me. It is the first I have ever won [as a manager]. It means something to our players, and they are with me in my stand. We never stopped until we clinched the pennant, even if it did rob the game of the interest of a pennant race. The club never complained. When the fight was hot we played to thousands. After the race was won we played to hundreds. But that was square sport and the stockholders never complained. If we didn't sacrifice our race in our own league to the box office we certainly are not going to put in jeopardy the highest honor in baseball simply for the box office inducements.

McGraw knew firsthand how the honor of a pennant can be lost in a postseason championship series. He had horrible memories of the pennant-winning Orioles of 1894 and 1895 losing the Temple Cup Series two straight years. McGraw and his teammates heard many hurtful remarks from the baseball public. "Fake champions!" "Quitters!" and "Can't take it when the chips are down!" are the ones he and his wife remembered. McGraw reacted very badly. "John went to bed," Blanche McGraw wrote, "and under a doctor's care for the rest of the year. At first his affliction was called nervousness, a sort of breakdown, and then it was diagnosed as malaria. He was weak, had recurring fever and regular head-aches." The situation in 1904—the possibility of losing the glory he always needed to a Ban Johnson American League team, and perhaps the hated New York rival at that—was dangerously similar to the one he could not handle in the 1890s. Was he going to chance it? The answer was no!

The baseball press did not think much of McGraw's statement. The *Chicago Sunday Tribune*, typically, thought it "makes him ridiculous. He practically admits the Giants would be defeated in such a series. . . . Truly McGraw must be hard pressed by public opinion when he makes 'breaks' like that." The *New York World* chastised McGraw for "entirely ignoring the almost unanimous opinion of the baseball public that the Giants should play either Boston or the Highlanders for the honors won last year by the Boston team," and added that "a careful perusal of his letter fails to show a reason of any kind, good or bad, for the stand he has taken. . . ." The *New York Daily Tribune* concurred: "What the baseball public, not only in this city but throughout the country, wishes now is a meeting of the winning teams of the National and American Leagues."

But nothing was going to change the minds of Brush and McGraw, not even a petition signed by 10,000 New York fans. What they did do, as an answer to criticism, was to bar the very outspoken Sam Crane, veteran newspaperman and former major league infielder, from the Polo Grounds. Back in the 1890s, in Cincinnati, Brush tried a similar punitive tactic when he took the press pass away from a troublesome sports editor named Ban Johnson. He didn't accomplish anything then either.

St. Louis was the site of the penultimate series for the Highlanders. When they left Sportsman's Park on October 5, they trailed the Pilgrims by half a game. They were coming back East for the last five games on their schedule to play their season-long archrivals from Boston. Three out of five is what they needed for the American League flag: win the series, win the pennant.

If "Dame Fortune" operates on an even-up basis, the Highlanders would have things their way back home because they sure weren't having much luck leaving the West. For hours, they sat on the train because of a wreck on the line at Terre Haute, Indiana. Finally, Griffith was able to switch his players to a second line, but because of the time lost, they arrived in New York only three hours before game time. Sharing the early portion of this frustrating journey with the Highlanders was New York's Governor Benjamin Odell, who, upon reaching Albany, sent a telegram to Griffith:

> Despite your running away from our sweeping challenge for a way station championship and laurels of our special train, the undersigned hope you and your splendid athletes of the diamond defeat the wily Boston beaneaters and achieve the world's championship as well as the American League pennant, for the great Empire State and for the City of New York. Foxily you hired a special train and ran away from us—worse than John T. Brush. However, the Gubernatorial staff admire your pluck and grand playing, and sincerely hope you win the big American League race.

When the Highlanders' brief rest ended in the early afternoon of Friday, October 7, and the opening contest with the Pilgrims at Hilltop Park was to begin, it was Jack Chesbro (40–10)—who else?—who got the call. According to *Sporting Life*, Chesbro told Griffith that, if necessary, he would work every day of the upcoming week. Facing him would be Norwood Gibson (17–13). Although Gibson had pitched exceptionally well lately, the New Yorkers might have been swinging against their old teammate Jesse Tannehill (21–11, 2.04ERA) had he not suffered a strained groin in Cleveland in late September and been forced to leave the club for the season.

The visitors drew first blood in the top of the third. With two out, "Kip" Selbach hit a roller just wide of shortstop "Kid" Elberfeld, so that although he made a fine stop on the ball, he could not throw it. When catcher "Red" Kleinow could not handle a Chesbro spitter, Selbach moved into scoring position. Freddy Parent then blooped one in front of center fielder John Anderson, and Selbach chased home with the game's initial score. The Highlanders, in their half of the inning, came right back. Elberfeld was hit by a Gibson pitch and scored on Anderson's double down the left field line. Two innings later, Patsy Dougherty led off with a flare that fell between Parent, the shortstop, and Selbach, the left fielder. Keeler, still playing with a bandaged right forefinger as a result of being hit by a pitched ball a week before, then slapped a ground ball to manager-third baseman Jimmy Collins, who got the throw over to first in time, but "Candy" LaChance could not hold on, creating a second and third situation for the Highlanders. Elberfeld followed with a fly ball to right, driving in New York's second run. In the bottom of the seventh, the Highlanders added a third tally: Dougherty reached first on another LaChance error, advanced to second on a base on balls to Elberfeld and crossed the plate on a single to left by Jimmy Williams. Although the Pilgrims got one more in the eighth, the tired hometown heroes hung on for a tremendously important triumph. "That the 'rooters' appreciated the work of Chesbro," reported *The New York Times*, "was shown after the last Boston man [catcher "Duke"] Farrell, was thrown out at first by Conroy. Rushing pell mell on the field, they picked the 'Happy One' up and carried him down the field to the clubhouse amid the wildest enthusiasm." Actually, both pitchers deserved special attention, each allowing but 4 hits. However, the 3–2 edge in runs gave Chesbro win number 41 and his New York team first place by half a game. "HIGHLANDERS HOME AND TAKE THE LEAD," announced the *New York World*.

It now looks as if the title of "World's Champions," so coveted by baseball players, will be passed over to the Highlanders by Monday afternoon next. The teams have four more games to play. Boston must win three of them to retain the championship, while an even break will suit the Highlanders.

"Nothing is easy in war," wrote Dwight Eisenhower. "Mistakes are always paid for in casualties. . . ." Back in mid-July, the Highlander management agreed to allow the Columbia University football team to use Hilltop Park for its October 8 game against Williams. At the time, the Highlanders trailed the first-place Pilgrims by 3½ games, with half the season to go. It did not seem incredibly significant that the baseball game scheduled for Hilltop that afternoon would have to be shifted elsewhere. But, by October 8, the single game had become a double-header, and the significance had become tremendous. The Highlanders had moved ahead of the Pilgrims by a half-game, thanks to their home victory on Friday, October 7, with 4 games left in the war for the American League banner. Now, thanks to that casual decision made nearly three months before, the critical Saturday double-header was to be transferred—to Boston! What this meant to those who knew the atmosphere pervading the Huntington Avenue Grounds was the very real possibility of a total shift in fate for the New York club. Over on Boston's Columbia Avenue, near Ruggles Street, was a Roxbury saloon run by Michael T. McGreevy, known as "Nuf Sed" to all the locals. The nickname came about because, as Pittsburg third baseman Tommy Leach heard it, "any time there was an argument about anything to do with baseball, he was the ultimate authority. Once McGreevy gave his opinion that ended the argument: nuf sed!" McGreevy headed a large group of Pilgrim fans who called themselves the "Royal Rooters." But these were not just fans. In fact, these were not just enthusiastic fans. These were monstrous, dominating, indefatigable, deciding fans. Tommy Leach believed that these "Royal Rooters" actually won the 1903 World Series for the Boston Pilgrims:

> We beat them three out of the first four games, and then they started singing that damn "Tessie" song. . . . They must have figured it was a good luck charm, because from then on you could hardly play ball they were singing "Tessie" so damn loud.
> "Tessie" was a real big popular song in those days. . . .
> "Tessie, you make me feel so badly,
> Why don't you turn around.
> Tessie, you know I love you madly,
> Babe, my heart weighs about a pound. . . ."
> Only instead of singing "Tessie, you know I love you madly," they'd sing special lyrics to each of the Red Sox players: like "Jimmy [Collins], you know I love you madly." And for us Pirates they'd change it a little. Like when Honus Wagner came up to bat they'd sing:
> "Honus, why do you hit so badly,
> Take a back seat and sit down.
> Honus, at bat you look so sadly,
> Hey, why don't you get out of town."
> Sort of got on your nerves after a while. And before we knew what happened, we'd lost the World Series.

Thirty thousand Bostonians showed up on Saturday, October 8, for this relocated double-header, and several thousands gathered around the downtown newspaper offices to keep track of the score. Every reserved seat had been sold the previous week, and the bleachers were packed an hour and a half before the action was to begin. Temporary seats were erected in front of the grandstand so that several hundred more could be squeezed in, but fans directed to this section blocked the view of those in the permanent boxes, causing such an outcry that some of the newly positioned benches had to be quickly removed. Still the rooters poured in, necessitating the opening of the field for standing areas. So close to the outfielders were the standees that it was agreed that anything hit fair into their roped-off midst would be a ground-rule double. Incredibly, the native of North Adams, Massachusetts, Jack Chesbro, with less than twenty-four hours rest, was to pitch again for New York. Facing him would be last year's World Series hero, Bill Dinneen. This was Chesbro's 50th start, one-third of his team's total games this season. However, the hard work did not appear to bother him through the first three innings. At this point, the Highlanders owned the only run, ex-Pilgrim Dougherty scoring that one. Then, in the Boston fourth, the fatigue Chesbro must have felt began to show. Six hits, a base on balls, and errors by Dougherty and Elberfeld cost the visitors 6 runs. Into the fray came Walter Clarkson, but the former ace of nearby Harvard College did no better, giving up 2 runs in the fifth, 4 in the sixth, and 1 in the seventh. At the end of this first game, the score read 13–2 and the American League standings showed Boston by a half-game over New York.

The second game's pitchers were Jack Powell and "Cy" Young. This would be a darkness-halted seven-inning contest, with only 1 run being registered. The lone tally occurred in the bottom of the fifth. Pilgrim second baseman Albert "Hobe" Ferris pushed a little grounder over second which Williams reached but could not convert. Catcher Lou Criger sacrificed Ferris to second. "Cy" Young then helped his own cause by smacking one deep enough to right to permit Ferris to tag up. When third baseman Conroy failed to handle Keeler's throw, allowing the ball to roll into the crowd, Ferris was waved home amid deafening cheers. Regarding Young's shutout performance, Jacob C. Morse wrote in *Sporting Life* that "nothing finer has been chronicled than the work of our 'grand old man' . . . who keeps on pitching

famous ball, despite the attempts to write him out of it. . . ."
Actually, something finer had been "chronicled" by Young
earlier in the year—a perfect game against the Philadelphia
Athletics. The all-time leader in games won, an astounding
511, had much written about him, including a little pan-
egyric by Grantland Rice:

> Fame may be fleeting and glory may fade—
> Life at its best is a breath on the glade.
> One hero passes, another is made,
> New stars arise as the old ones pale.
> So when a stalwart steps out from the throng
> On with the tribute, let garlands be flung—
> Here's to the king of them all, Denton True Young.

The Highlanders now trailed by 1½ games. "I am still
confident we will land the flag," Clark Griffith told the press,
"and the boys are too. Chesbro will go against the champions
on Monday. He usually does that when he has been hit hard,
and turns the tables. We are all cheerful."

The two clubs had Sunday to travel back to New York,
repair and dry out their ripped and sweat-soaked uniforms,
and rest up for the double-header on Monday, the last day of
the season. Accompanying the Pilgrims were 200 "Royal
Rooters," prepared to do to the Highlanders what they had
done to the Pirates the previous year. On the rear of the
railroad car that they stuffed themselves into was a banner
that read: "WE WANT THESE TWO GAMES. 'NUF SED.' " When
they reached New York, they headed for the Hotel Marl-
borough, where they joyously milled about, sporting red
badges with the words "WORLD'S CHAMPIONS" written
across. *The New York Times* noted that "quite a number of the
visitors carried suit cases and satchels which they took with
them to Pittsburg last fall 'just for luck.' " The word at the

hotel was that Dinneen and Chesbro, as Griffith had promised, would be the pitchers in the first game. "The Boston
men," said the *Times*, "think Chesbro has been worked too
hard, and that the drubbing he got on Saturday marked the
beginning of his down fall." New York City was electric with
excitement over the American League showdown. "Probably
no such interest ever was taken in a baseball event in this
city," thought the *Times*.

Monday, October 10, began with threatening weather but
cleared up by the time the crowd of 28,584 lucky ticket
holders pushed through the entrance gates of Hilltop Park.
The "Royal Rooters" positioned themselves at the extreme left
of the grandstand. They brought along the Lew Dockstader's
Band, which, together with the megaphones and tin horns
held to many agitated mouths, kept up a continuous din
throughout the ball game. "Tessie" was on hand, also. One of
the "Rooters" stood above the Boston bench and led his
comrades in the rallying tune until, the *Boston Herald* noted,
"the performers must have been as tired as the auditors,
some of whom inquired innocently enough if that was the
only air the band could play."

Chesbro hadn't lost much in 1904—in fact, only 11 times
in 52 decisions—and after 4 of those times, he bounced right
back to take the next contest from the team that did him in.
Today, in the first game, he could make it 5 quick avengings
with a triumph over Boston. "I am willing to bet my last
dollar that I trim Collins' boys," he told the *New York World*.
And so it appeared that trimming was what he was up to
when the first three Pilgrims he faced were retired in order.
Patsy Dougherty led off the Highlander half with a base on
balls and took second on a Willie Keeler sacrifice. However,
neither "Kid" Elberfeld nor Jimmy Williams was able to cash
in this potential run, and the game was scoreless after one. In
the second, "Buck" Freeman and "Hobe" Ferris singled, but
were left stranded by Lou Criger. When John Anderson,

John Ganzel, and "Wid" Conroy went down quietly in the second against Bill Dinneen, this crucial game showed all the signs of being exactly what it should be: a classic pitchers' duel. Ground balls got rid of Dinneen and "Kip" Selbach in the third, and Chesbro, for the second time, struck out Freddy Parent. After "Red" Kleinow continued the afternoon's dismal hitting exhibition by grounding out to begin the Highlander third, Chesbro stepped to the plate. Time, however, was called. At this point, it was decided to allow "Happy Jack's" fans to present him with a fur overcoat and cap. "He'll strike out for sure on account of that fur overcoat," predicted a superstitious fan within earshot of the *New York Herald*'s reporter. "But," the reporter wrote, "Chesbro this time made an exception in the case of players who go to bat and do nothing after having received a present. He slammed the ball along the right field line for three bases." With Chesbro ninety feet away from a New York lead, Dougherty and Keeler—the most consistent hitters in the Highlander line-up—did something not even the most loyal Pilgrim krank could have expected: they both struck out. Still, Griffith could take heart at the way Chesbro was pitching. He seemed to be getting stronger as the struggle progressed. Dinneen, on the other hand, faltered in the bottom of the fifth. Although he got Ganzel and Conroy out, Kleinow singled sharply to right and Chesbro smashed one right back through the middle past Dinneen. Dougherty, who had a knack for heroics, followed with a line single to right, driving in Kleinow with the first run of the game. Shaken by 3 straight hard hits, Dinneen proceeded to walk Keeler to fill the bases—perhaps he just didn't want to pitch to him anyhow. "Such cheering!" declared the *New York Herald*. "One had to stuff cotton in his ears in order to think. The cheering became a roar when Elberfeld walked, forcing Chesbro over the plate." But the fun ended there as Williams hit softly back to Dinneen for the long-delayed third out. Two runs constituted a good lead, with Chesbro doing his thing on the mound. However, despite the attention pitchers naturally get, it is a fact that they cannot win all by themselves. This basic baseball truth was made evident in the top of the seventh. Chesbro got 2 strikes on "Candy" LaChance, but the big first baseman reached out and poked the next pitch just over Chesbro's head. Second baseman "Buttons" Williams got to the ball but couldn't make the throw in time. Ferris, the next hitter, chopped a routine ground ball directly at Williams, who just couldn't find the handle. Criger advanced both runners with a fine sacrifice bunt. Pitcher Bill Dinneen seemed to be helping Chesbro out of this mess when he followed with another routine grounder to Williams, who fielded this one all right, but then fired the ball into the dirt in front of catcher Kleinow, allowing both runners to score and even the contest, 2–2. Williams' poor play had allowed Boston to get untracked and put the game up for grabs. In the top of the eighth, Charley "Chick" Stahl, Freeman, and LaChance got hits, and Boston was poised to jump into the lead. However, the Highlander defense came to the rescue, cutting down Stahl at the plate on a pretty relay play from center fielder Anderson to shortstop Elberfeld to Kleinow. So, toe to toe, Boston and New York went into the ninth inning looking for that little opening that would allow the deciding blow to land. In the top half of the inning, slow-footed, weak-hitting (.208) Lou Criger beat out a roller to short. Dinneen did his job, sacrificing Criger to second. Selbach, at the top of the line-up, was in a storybook position to bring home his relatively new club a winner, but Chesbro threw that spitter of his and "Kip" tapped the ball back to the mound. This made 2 outs, with Criger still on third. The second spot on the Boston card belonged to shortstop Freddy Parent. Twice this day Parent was a strikeout victim. And, for all the world, it appeared that Parent was about to go down a third time when Chesbro blew 2 strikes past the little 5-foot-5½-inch guy on the first 2 pitches. The "Book" says that an 0–2 count calls for a pitch out of the strike zone to make the hitter, who is in an extremely defensive position, swing at something he cannot hit solidly. Was the next toss by Chesbro a "waste pitch"? What is known is that it was one of his spitballs and that it was high, wild, and beyond Kleinow's reach. Back it went to the foot of the grandstand and in trotted Criger with the go-ahead run. Although Parent hit the next pitch into center field for a single, that does not necessarily mean that the run would have scored anyway because game conditions, including pressure and pitching strategy, would have been different and such things clearly have great effects on performance. So, although no more damage was done, the visitors were up that big one tally, 3–2, and it all came down to what the home team could do in its "last licks." Ganzel, the number six hitter, darkened the already gloomy picture for the New Yorkers by striking out for the second consecutive time. But then Conroy drew a walk. Next came Kleinow, who had 2 hits this game. However, he popped out to second baseman Ferris. Chesbro's spot in the order had been reached. What were the Highlanders to do in this critical situation? Chesbro, too, had 2 hits off Dinneen, including that post-fur–overcoat–gift triple. The 1904 season had been Chesbro's best as a hitter (.236 average) as well as a pitcher. But, this was the most important at-bat of the Highlanders' season, and it could not go to a pitcher. Griffith made a move. Hitting for Chesbro would be Jim McGuire. The "Deacon," however, was hitting only .210 and was unlikely to beat out an infield hit if it should come to that. Nevertheless, the substitution paid off in that the patient veteran catcher worked Dinneen for a walk, sending Conroy to second as the tying run. The line-up turned over to the top of the order. What a spot for Dougherty, the former Pilgrim left fielder. He could have the sweetest revenge baseball offers: snatching away the pennant from the organization that traded him. Patsy was hitting .279 and already had an RBI this afternoon. Meanwhile, Dave Fultz went out to run for McGuire at first. The dramatic tension couldn't be any higher—but it wasn't sustained long: three pitches, and nothing but air! Dougherty struck out. "No man in this land wanted to have the Highlanders humble the champions as much as Dougherty did. Then to be finally out-generaled by his ex-clubmates with two men on bases waiting to be brought home—it was simply awful," commented the *New York World* with appropriate sympathy. Suddenly, it was all over. What had been a seemingly endless and gut-wrenching war, requiring triumph after triumph, had ended in the flash of one empty swing. Conroy, who would have been mobbed with supreme joy under other circumstances, walked dejectedly toward the clubhouse. The facts were brutal in their simplicity and would admit no change: the Highlanders had come in second and the Pilgrims had won their second American League pennant in a row. The "Royal Rooters" were delirious. They, the Lew Dockstader's Band, and other Bostonians in town celebrated with a torchlight parade down Broadway. What a humiliating scene that was for the proud Highlanders and their loyal supporters.

There was a second game that day, which the Highlanders won, 1–0, in extra innings, behind Ambrose Puttman. "Today, after the first game of the doubleheader had been won by Boston," wrote T. E. Sanborn in *The Sporting News,*

> there was absolutely no reason for playing the second game, as nothing depended on it. McGraw and his Giants would undoubtedly have made a farce of it and driven the patrons away. Not so the Bostons and Highlanders. They fought out a 10-inning game as sharply as if it mattered who won it and showed the kind of spirit that wins baseball fans of all degrees.

But, aside from showing "class" in playing despite a

shattered spirit, it really did not matter to the Highlanders. The real issue had been decided in the ninth inning of the first game. That loss was to be a demon that destroyed all the pleasure Jack Chesbro should have derived from his dazzling 1904 season. He had started 51 games and completed 48 of them, pitched 454.2 innings, posted a 41–12 record, and finished with a 1.82 ERA—and all he could think about was that wild pitch, what has been called the most costly wild pitch in history. Several weeks after the close of the season, Chesbro and Griffith went on a hunting trip. Lee Allen tells the poignant story:

> "Why don't you look for something to shoot?" Griffith said to him in the woods.
> "I was thinking," Chesbro replied.
> "About that wild pitch?"
> "Yes."
> "Now, look here," Griff said. "If you ever mention that wild pitch again, I'll shoot you as I would a muskrat. Now shut up and hunt."

But Chesbro could not forget and neither, later, could his widow, who attempted to blame "Red" Kleinow for letting it get behind him. Fred Lieb asked "Kid" Elberfeld about the possibility of Kleinow catching that infamous pitch. Elberfeld exploded: "The only way Kleinow could have caught that ball would have been while standing on top of a stepladder." "Deacon" McGuire, who caught two-thirds of the Highlander games that year, was asked if he might have been able to grab "the wild pitch." "There wasn't a chance of stopping that spitter," he asserted. "It might as well have gone over the top of the grandstand."

But the criticisms and "what ifs" of baseball are part of its great fun and provide good kindling for the long "hot-stove league" season. The winter of 1904–05 would be much longer and much less satisfying than the last because there was no World Series to analyze over and over again. One final try—probably to taunt the Giant management—had been made by Pilgrim owner John Taylor, when, on October 10, he announced an offer for a series of games between the two championship teams, with all the receipts to be divided among the players. According to the *Boston Herald,* a number of the top Giant players would have leaped at the chance. The journal reported that at the deciding Pilgrim-Highlander double-header, McGinnity complained that "it is just like taking money out of our pockets to prevent us from playing the winners. The players are willing enough, I tell you. I think McGraw has the best ball tossers ever got together and I think they can beat any aggregation when in trim." Then, he added, "Of course, they are out of training now, and cannot play the ball they did two months ago."

The "Royal Rooters," in their special fashion, made it known that they wanted a chance to see their Pilgrims play the Giants. As they left Hilltop Park for their hotel, they carried two brooms supporting a long banner that read: "Mr. Brush, we're on plush. Where are you? Don't be vain. Give us a game." Nevertheless, there was a benefit for the Boston club in the Giant management's stubbornness. As the *New York World's* headline proclaimed: "THE BOSTONS STILL HOLD TITLE OF WORLD CHAMPIONS, GIANTS REFUSING TO PLAY." "As there is no challenge for the greater title," the journal explained, "Jimmy Collins's men will retain it for another year. Possibly in 1905 the National League winners may at least try to take the honors from the Boston boys."

Epilogue

The game itself, in 1904, did not depart from the era's style of play, regulations, conditions, and mores. Fielders played on poor surfaces using tiny gloves and made many errors trying to catch and throw a pounded "dead ball." Pitching staffs relied on three or four workhorses who were expected to finish their two-hour games and generally did. "Inside baseball" tactics, which governed the offense from the first inning on, required that the lead-off hitter get on any way he could—even if that meant "taking one for the team"; that he be advanced by a sacrifice or hit-and-run or, failing this, that he steal; and that he be moved around and score by well-placed singles, a fly ball, or a squeeze play. Extremely large grounds made it difficult to reach the fences, so many home runs were inside the park. There was no such thing as platooning or righty-lefty strategy switches. The few substitutes on the roster hardly ever pinch-hit or pinch-ran, but simply waited around for an injury to a regular for a few days' playing time. Managers—often playing managers—treated their players

harshly, but not as harshly as they and their players treated
the lone umpire. Fans—"kranks"—were very active and vo-
cal, and, when they outnumbered the grandstand and
bleachers seats, could be found a few feet away from the
players behind ropes in the spacious outfield and all the way
down the foul lines. Double-headers were used to draw large
holiday crowds and fit in games that were previously rained
out or called on account of darkness. Frequently, at the end
of the season, these make-up double-headers had to be
played back to back.

However, the 1904 season had its very special features,
too, the most significant of them involving teams from New
York City. Even before the season began, the New York
clubs, the old Giants and the new Highlanders, clashed over
the scheduling of games to the degree that the year-old peace
that halted the extremely intense "Great Baseball War" between the American and National leagues seemed threatened. This dispute revealed the tremendous desire on the
part of both leagues to win the loyalties of baseball fans in
Manhattan. But, beyond the naturally strong competition
between teams playing in the same general section of the
same small island, there was the unnaturally bitter hatred
between the president of the American League, Ban
Johnson, and the directors of the New York National League
club, owner John Brush and manager John McGraw. This
deeply personal animus stemmed from old quarrels that
took grotesque shape in other cities—Cincinnati and Baltimore—and expanded to dimensions that shattered all civil
discourse between them. Brush and McGraw so hated and
despised Johnson and the successful Highlander team he
slipped into New York that they could not accept the possibility of losing a postseason challenge that would leave
their rivals "World Champions." The result was that the
Giants set their sights exclusively on winning the National
League flag, virtually disbanded their winning combination

in late September, and were in no position to play the Boston Pilgrims, who defeated the Highlanders on the last day of the season for the American League pennant—even if they wanted to. Because of the Giants' degeneration, there is no reason to believe that the Giant management would be willing to chance playing a World Series even with some club other than the Highlanders. Brush had never accepted the existence of the American League in anything but the most formal of ways; and McGraw, a successful manager for the first time, appears to have been plagued by his old Temple Cup memories of losing all the accolades earned over a whole season by quirky misfortune in a short championship series. In brief, the reputedly tough-as-nails businessman Brush and athlete McGraw shrank back from the 1904 World Series because of ulcerous hatreds, organizational overprotection, and strong personal fears. Neither would risk giving Ban Johnson his greatest triumph. Both remembered the unhappy fate of the 1903 National League Pittsburg Pirates in their confrontation with the American League Boston Pilgrims. And both were too pleased with the consensus that their Giants represented one of the finest teams in baseball history to gamble on hot pitchers and bats over two weeks of extended play. For McGraw there was the additional consideration of a victorious Clark Griffith. If "the Old Fox" turned out to be the manager of the World Champion Highlanders, then Johnson would have been vindicated in his 1902 decision of Griffith and not McGraw for the field leadership of the New York American League club. So many wounds, so many raw nerve endings, so many distended egos—just too many for there to have been a World Series in 1904.

Nevertheless, even though Ban Johnson's organization was deprived of the opportunity to defeat the Giants in October, it had won a great victory at the gate and in the press in September. A delicious irony enjoyed by the American League president was that the decision by Brush and

McGraw to deny the Highlanders a chance to capture the New York baseball audience through a World Series victory resulted in a great outpouring of sympathetic feeling on the part of fans and journalists for the dogged squad from Washington Heights. Starting with Friday, September 23, the first game following their pennant clincher, the Giants played fourteen games on ten separate dates (including one Saturday and three weekday double-headers), all at the home Polo Grounds. Altogether, they drew 34,198 fans—an average of 2,443 per game. At the same time, the Highlanders played eighteen games on fourteen separate dates (including one Saturday, one Sunday, and two weekday double-headers), all but three of these games on the road in Cleveland, Detroit, Chicago, St. Louis, and Boston. Altogether, they drew 133,127 fans—an average of 7,396 per game. The lesson was clear—the "kranks" wanted to see significant action, games that meant something. The Highlanders, snubbed by Brush and McGraw, were playing for the American League pennant. The Giants could have been getting ready for the World Series—that would have meant something special to their very loyal following. Whereas 9,198 Giant fans came out to see them play Pittsburg on Saturday, September 24, at the beginning of this stretch of late-season games, only 300 came out to see them play the St. Louis Cardinals on October 3, at the end when they had prematurely packed it in. An enthusiastic crowd of 56,525 Bostonians and New Yorkers came to the last two double-headers between the Pilgrims and the Highlanders. Johnson's cause was literally enriched by these excited spectators, each of whom, along with many others across the baseball world, held the Giant management in enormous contempt.

In fact, John Brush took so much abuse over his and John McGraw's ill-advised temper tantrum that through the winter of 1904–05, he decided to clear the air and take the lead in devising a permanent arrangement for a postseason championship series between the major leagues that still serves as a basic model. The so-called "Brush Rules," adopted in the spring of 1905, called for a four-of-seven-game competition, with 60 percent of the receipts from the first four contests going to the players: 75 percent of this figure to the winners and 25 percent to the losers. The National Baseball Commission was to receive 10 percent and the remaining 30 percent was to be divided by the two participating organizations. Players had to be on the active team roster prior to September 1 to be eligible. Finally, each club had to post a $10,000 bond, guaranteeing fulfillment of all stipulated conditions—this would keep an owner from suddenly calling off any future World Series! As baseball historian David Voigt notes, "This important agreement stabilized relations between the two leagues and went far to end the guerrilla warfare that marked the early years of the National Agreement."

Brush lived for another eight years, but not at all well. He suffered from locomotor ataxia, which progressively disabled him and finally put him in a wheelchair. In 1911, he sat in his wheelchair and watched the Polo Grounds burn down. Rather than rebuild the old wooden ballpark, Brush turned this unfortunate event into an opportunity by building a concrete and steel enclosure that rivaled the two such existing structures, Forbes Field in Pittsburgh and Shibe Park in Philadelphia. From 1911 to 1919, the new Polo Grounds would be officially called "Brush Stadium." However, the Giant owner would not see very many games at his new ballpark. In the summer of 1912, he broke his hip, and, shortly thereafter, on his way to California aboard his private railroad car, just west of St. Louis, he suffered a fatal stroke. Mrs. Elsie Lombard Brush and John's two daughters, Eleanor, from his first marriage, and Natalie were left the Giants (placed under the control of his son-in-law Harry Hempstead), his millions, his department store and a large home in Indianapolis, another large home in Florida, and an estate in New Jersey. Not a bad legacy for a poor orphan from central New York who fought his way through the Civil War and up the ladder of the business worlds of clothing and baseball. Unfortunately, an intimate look at his life was made extremely difficult by the protective action of his daughter Eleanor (Mrs. Hempstead), who, right after his death, destroyed all his private papers.

On the way up the business and baseball ladders, Brush antagonized many, if not most, of those who felt him treading past without much concern for their welfare or sensibilities. However, one he did not antagonize was John Joseph McGraw. Brush was always exceedingly good to his field leader and never interfered with his baseball decisions. McGraw was, in effect, the "general manager" as well as the manager of the Giants. At Brush's funeral, McGraw noted the physical suffering the man had gone through and added that, nevertheless, "he was there at all times when it came to the transaction of the great big business of life. This is a great battle, this battle of life. What a wonderful, what a beautiful character was John Brush." McGraw's fondness for Brush stemmed directly from the fact that, in the "battle" of baseball life, Brush and McGraw were always on the same side—and the joint decision to call off the 1904 World Series provided the early seal on this union of purpose and will that suffered no discernible cracks for the decade of their association. If the Giants' baseball battles weren't always won under the severely centralized McGraw direction—the power structure that Brush allowed to be established—they were hardly ever out of hand. After the 1904 pennant, the McGraw Giants won nine more, three in a row (1911–13) and then four more in a row (1921–24), finished second ten times, and finished in the second division on only three occasions. In 1905, the first year of the new "Brush Rules," the Giants defeated the Philadelphia Athletics in the World Series, four games to one. And in the 1921 and 1922 World Series, McGraw's club defeated the New York Yankees five games to three and four games to none. Only Connie Mack guided his team to more regular season victories than John McGraw, and this because Mack managed twenty years longer. In 1937, the Baseball Writers' Association of America, voting for the second time on membership in the Hall of Fame (officially dedicated in June 1939), selected John McGraw as worthy of joining the original five: Ty Cobb, "Babe" Ruth, "Honus" Wagner, Walter Johnson, and his old pitcher and friend Christy Mathewson.

McGraw's long career had an enormous impact on people in the game. His extreme martinetlike managerial style is legendary. "With my team," he declared, and meant it, "I'm absolute czar. I order plays and they obey. If they don't, I fine them." In 1915, infielder Sammy Strang was asked to lay down a sacrifice bunt; instead he hit a home run over the left field wall. After he touched all the bases and trotted to the bench, all smiles, he was confronted by McGraw and reminded about the bunt instructions. "But it was right in there," responded Strang. "It looked so inviting I just had to take a poke at it." "You did, huh," rumbled the McGraw rejoinder. "Well, I hope it's worth it because it'll cost you 25 bucks." There were those who couldn't play for McGraw because of this uncompromising approach. Hall of Fame outfielder Eddie Roush hated his three years with the Giants:

Me, I didn't like New York. I'm a small-town boy. I like the Midwest. Well, it wasn't exactly that. Not entirely, anyway. It was really McGraw I didn't like. John J. McGraw. I just didn't enjoy playing for him, that's all. If you made a bad play he'd cuss you out, yell at you, call you all sorts of names. That didn't go with me. So I was glad as I could be when he traded me to Cincinnati in the middle of the '16 season. I couldn't have been happier.

And Bob O'Farrell, who caught in the major leagues for twenty-one years with a number of teams, didn't remember his four with McGraw fondly either:

> Now McGraw, he was rough as a manager. Very hard to play for. I played for him from '28 to '32, when he retired, and I didn't like it. You couldn't seem to do anything right for him, ever. If something went wrong it was always your fault, not his. . . . No, McGraw was never a very cheerful man to be around. At least, that's my opinion.

Yet, he had his loyal supporters, too. Shortstop Al Bridwell, who also played for McGraw for four years, remembered him as

> a wonderful man, a real fighter, that's what he was. He'd argue with the umpires, the opposing players, the people in the stands. Anybody wanted to argue, he was ready. I got along with him fine. He only suspended me once, for two weeks. It was on account of I socked him.
>
> Well, I didn't really sock him. It was more of a push. I pushed him, sort of, and he fell down the dugout steps. Well, maybe it was a sock at that. . . .
>
> What happened was that I missed a sign. . . . When I got back to the dugout he called me a lot of names and so I hit him. He suspended me for two weeks without pay, but once it was over he forgot about it completely. Never mentioned it again. He was a fighter, but he was also the kindest, best-hearted fellow you ever saw. I liked him and I liked playing for him. . . . He knew how to handle men. Some players he rode, and others he didn't. He got the most out of each man. It wasn't so much knowing baseball. All of them know that. One manager knows about as much about the fundamentals of baseball as another. What makes the difference is knowing each player and how to handle him. And at that sort of thing nobody came anywhere close to McGraw.

Actually, Bridwell was right, there was a soft side to McGraw. For one thing, he felt a bond with former players who were down and out, and gave them work around the ballpark as watchmen, gate attendants, and groundskeepers. When, in 1908 Fred Merkle, in his second year as a Giant first baseman, failed to touch second base, thereby forcing his team into a losing play-off game against Chicago that cost the pennant, McGraw, surprisingly, not only kept his notorious temper but showed tremendous compassion. He carefully rebuilt the young man's confidence verbally and even gave him a modest raise in the following year's contract. McGraw explained what some criticized as an inconsistent treatment of his players in an article in *Literary Digest:* "Learn to know every man under you, get under his skin, know his faults. Then cater to him—with kindness or roughness, as his case may demand." His selective decency didn't just extend to certain fortunate baseball players. He was that way with the press and the public, too. "Did you ever meet him?" one sportswriter asked his readers.

> Did you ever come face to face and shake hands with the most unpopular man in the baseball business? If you did, the first thing that crosses your mind is that the person who introduced you is putting up a joke on you. It doesn't seem possible that the mild-mannered, gentlemanly, quiet man who shakes your hand is John McGraw. I have seen this John McGraw time and time again give up his lower berth or his stateroom on a trip to a woman and her children who had an upper or perhaps no berth at all. I have seen him do the same for an old man—and then sit up all night in the smoker.

What McGraw wanted most, after winning, was to make the Giants the sharpest baseball operation in the major leagues. He would never allow his club to be outdone if he could at all help it, and this went for everything from training facilities to field and clubhouse maintenance to off-season opportunities. The controversial world tour with Jim Hart's Chicago Colts, announced late in the 1904 season, never did occur. In truth, it was meant to be no more than a way to dodge the World Series. However, a decade later, in a much changed baseball environment, John McGraw and Charley Comiskey of the Chicago White Sox arranged for a trip to distant and exotic places for their players. Leaving after the Philadelphia Athletics defeated the Giants four games to one in the 1913 World Series, the two clubs played their way across 38,000 miles, bringing their expert version of baseball to such places as Yokohama, Shanghai, Manila, Sydney, Cairo, Naples, Rome, Monte Carlo, London, and Paris. John McGraw, the poor, tough kid from Truxton, New York, got to meet Pope Pius X and King George V of England, as well as Japanese royalty, Australian governors, East Indian princes, khedives, and numerous ambassadors and military chiefs. The group then returned in March 1914 on the British passenger liner the *Lusitania*. Within five months Europe would be engaged in the Great War; and, in slightly more than a year, the *Lusitania* would be sunk by a German U-boat with 1,200 fatalities, 10 percent of them American.

McGraw's time hadn't come yet. But, by the early 1930s, he was no longer in good health. Forty games into the 1932 season, his doctors convinced him to hand over the field reins and remain as vice president only. This he did very reluctantly. The man he carefully chose to be manager of the Giants was Bill Terry, future Hall of Fame first baseman, then in his tenth year with the club, the last two of which were spent without exchanging a single friendly word with McGraw. In February 1934, at the age of sixty, suffering from prostate cancer and uremic poisoning in New Rochelle Hospital, John McGraw died.

Back in 1912, when McGraw's old friend John Brush was

on his deathbed, the archfoe of the Giant management team, American League President Ban Johnson, made a surprising visit, and an even more startling reconciliation took place. Johnson was then at the acme of his career and the power structure of organized baseball. In January 1913, *The Sporting News* published a front–page picture of Johnson, noting that he was "the dominant figure in the greatest power ever developed in any field of sport. He wields the 'big stick' as he sees fit for the men who employ him, the owners of the American League clubs. They have absolute faith in him, his word is law and they pay him $25,000 a year for life." According to Branch Rickey, one of the game's most respected and innovative executives, "Ban Johnson was the czar of baseball in America. He ruled the game." He was able to do this because of the two other members of the National Commission, one was the president of the National League—and this figure changed too often to allow for accumulated authority—and the other was Chairman Garry Herrmann, a personal friend who was willing to follow Johnson's more decisive opinions and courses of action.

Johnson worked hard at being "czar," sacrificing much of his home life with his wife Sara Jane—or "Jen," as he called her. They were married in 1892, and, after the American League was established, lived in a very modest, rented brick row house in Chicago, where Ban maintained his main office. Their childless, generally Spartan existence had a few corners of worldly weakness. Jen accepted jewelry in lieu of a warm family life. So enormous a collection did she amass that a separate auction had to be held to dispose of it after her death. Ban's distractions cut deeply into the strong Protestant values of his Ohio upbringing. For a time, after he was first married, he had an eye for pretty women; in later life, he often settled his nerves using a bottle of liquor. Apparently, he was at his worst during the World Series, when he really let loose. Journalist Fred Lieb recalled Ban's being drunk on many of these occasions, not "staggering drunk, but he had the shrill voice and unsteady manner of a drinking man."

More than thirty years at the top of any business, especially such a volatile and visible one as major league baseball, would naturally subject a person to many trying incidents. Certain of these incidents touched especially sensitive nerves and deserve special attention because of what they reveal about the man.

Late in 1913, two "outlaw" minor circuits called the United States League and the Columbian League—outlaw because they were outside the National Agreement—reorganized as the Federal League and had the temerity to declare itself a major league. It would play in six cities: Chicago, St. Louis, Cleveland, Pittsburgh (by this time the post office had reinserted the "h" in the spelling of this city's name), Covington (Cincinnati), and Indianapolis. All of this had to look more than vaguely familiar to Ban Johnson, who guided the metamorphosis of the American League from its original state as the minor Western League. Since the Federal League did not challenge the reserve clause at first, there seemed little cause for Ban Johnson to be greatly concerned. But when the "Feds" decided to ignore the reserve clause and sign any players they could get, and 221 experienced players, 81 of them from established major league clubs, jumped to the new league for higher salaries and a more liberal player relations policy, Johnson was furious: "I will not take a single man back who steps over the line dividing the American and Federal League. I hereby tell one and all of them that I will not even talk to them." Despite the fact that a little more than a decade before it was Johnson who was raiding the National League in an effort to create an authentic "big league" operation, he asserted righteously that there was no room for another circuit at the top level. As Fred Lieb remarked, "Oh, now he's in, and things look different than when you're outside looking in." For the second Federal League season, 1915, oilman Harry Sinclair came in as the financial backer of a new club scheduled to play in Newark, but it was clear that the club intended to move to New York City. This must have truly seemed to be a déjà vu situation for Ban Johnson. However, following the October 1915 death of Brooklyn franchise owner Robert B. Ward, one of the important personal and financial forces keeping the new circuit going, the Federal League was on the verge of collapse. Nevertheless, it had instituted a troublesome antitrust suit against organized baseball in the United States District Court for Northern Illinois, over which Judge Kenesaw Mountain Landis presided. Landis was a Theodore Roosevelt appointee who had already shown that he was not impressed with standing or power by calling John D. Rockefeller to Chicago to testify in a case against his Standard Oil Company. Curiously, Landis kept delaying his ruling on the antitrust suit. "Do you realize," he finally explained, "that a decision in this case may tear down the very foundations of this game, so loved by thousands, and do you realize that the decision must seriously affect both parties?" Landis's delay allowed Ban Johnson and the National Commission time to negotiate with the "Fed" leaders, and, with buy-outs and mergers arranged to everyone's satisfaction, the new league and the antitrust suit were ended. Johnson's lockout threat was lost in a general amnesty agreement and many major league players who had jumped to the "Feds" were immediately accepted back by their former American and National League clubs for the 1916 season.

Ban Johnson owed much to Charley Comiskey for his remarkable career. It was Comiskey, player-manager of the Cincinnati Reds who recommended Johnson to the failing Western League as the man who could save it; and it was Comiskey who, as the owner of the Chicago White Sox, worked very closely with the president of the new American

League to make his risky venture a solid and successful one. Take Comiskey out of the picture, and the biography of Ban Johnson might just be an interesting story of a leading American sports journalist. Not only were Comiskey and Johnson close with regard to their business interests, but they were "pals," too—at least for a long while. It wasn't any single thing but a collection of little things that changed a great friendship into a protracted hatred. The incidents began with a practical joke during a hunting trip. Someone—not Comiskey, although he was in the hunting party—placed blanks in Johnson's gun, and then the group accused him of drinking too much when he couldn't hit his targets. The hard feelings between the two got worse when Johnson suspended White Sox outfielder James "Ducky" Holmes at a time when Comiskey's club was short players. Johnson didn't inform Comiskey of his action until late, and then, embarrassingly, by proxy before a big Sunday crowd. Then there was the ruling on Jack Quinn, a pitcher Comiskey signed off a Pacific Coast League roster when that organization temporarily suspended play because of the draining effects of the World War I draft. Comiskey liked Quinn and wanted to re-sign him for the next season, but his old Pacific Coast League club had decided to sell him to the Yankees instead. The National Commission, obeying a previously established rule about who had title to what players, decided that the Yankees, and not Comiskey, would get Quinn's services. Of course, Comiskey held Johnson responsible for this decision, as he and most everyone else assumed that the National Commission was just a Johnson front. Then came the concluding chapter of the Johnson-Comiskey story, the one having to do with eight White Sox players who conspired with gamblers to throw the 1919 World Series to the Cincinnati Reds.

That something strange was occurring that fall was apparent from the morning of the first game, when, despite the strong consensus that the White Sox had the superior team, the odds suddenly favored the Reds. Veteran reporter Hugh Fullerton couldn't help but notice the amount of gambling activity going on in the lobby of the Metropole Hotel and told his colleague Fred Lieb, "Something's wrong. . . . I don't like it." Early on, White Sox manager "Kid" Gleason told Comiskey that he suspected a fix. Comiskey relayed this worrisome story to National League President John Heydler, who passed it along to Ban Johnson. Johnson's reaction was that Comiskey's complaint was nothing more than an excuse for his team's poor performance. "That's the yelp of a beaten cur!" he exclaimed with annoyance. In fact, Johnson later said that he sat through the entire series appalled at the White Sox play, but without the slightest notion of a conspiracy. If Johnson was being honest here, it was an admission that he was out of touch with the feelings of the baseball community. As Eugene Murdock states, "The tavern talk, the corridor conversation, and bits and snatches picked up by astute reporters pointed in no other direction" than that the fix was in. Yet, nothing official was done about the throwing of the 1919 World Series until stories began to surface again the following fall. Then came the official proceedings and the personal recriminations. Johnson accused Comiskey of being aware of the fix but failing to act forthrightly, and Comiskey charged that Johnson was trying to destroy his White Sox organization during its drive for the 1920 American League pennant. However, too much had been said and written to dodge the fix charge any further, and the matter was handed over to the courts and the owners for judgment. Ultimately, evidence from the grand jury files having been stolen, the trial of accused players and gamblers ended impotently with acquittals. With respect to baseball's management, the feeling on the part of the owners was that the three-man National Commission had shown unpardonable weakness, and that a more decisive structure capable of a more deliberate response to problems should be installed in its place. Reorganization of baseball's hierarchy had been discussed prior to the "Black Sox scandal," as it has come to be known, but the events of 1919–1920 gave a specific and powerful reason for the adoption of a new order.

In October 1920, baseball's owners dismissed the National Commission and established the commissioner's office. The man chosen as the game's single chief executive was Kenesaw Mountain Landis, the tough judge with the tender spot for baseball, as he exhibited during the Federal League's antitrust suit. Ban Johnson was retained as the American League president, but that was it. He was no longer "czar"; Landis was. Johnson had always been a proud man, and this seemed to be a situation in which a proud man would quit. But his dreary, childless home was not something he could run to for solace. The American League had become his whole life. Fred Lieb witnessed Johnson inebriated and sloppily sentimental, ranting over and over again about his creation, "the American League—the greatest institution in the country; the greatest institution in the world." So, he swallowed his pride and stayed on, drawing up the playing schedule, directing the umpires, and settling disputes as a court of semi-final resort.

In late 1926, Johnson was asked to exercise this last responsibility in a potentially explosive situation having to do with an accusation made by former Detroit pitcher Hubert "Dutch" Leonard. Leonard turned certain evidence over to Johnson suggesting that two of baseball's greatest hitters and outfielders, Detroit's Ty Cobb and Cleveland's Tris Speaker, also the club's manager, had, on September 24, 1919, met under the grandstand of Detroit's Navin Field and fixed the game to be played the following day. If the Tigers could win that contest, they would slide past the Yankees into third place, thereby earning a share of the money that went to the top three teams in the final standings in each league. Leonard and pitcher Joe Wood also placed bets on the sure-thing Tigers, with Cobb making the arrangements. As planned, Detroit defeated Cleveland, and Leonard and Wood made a quick and easy $130. By 1926, both Cobb and Speaker were in the very late stages of their illustrious careers, serving as players-managers for their old ball clubs. But Johnson could not tolerate the injury they had committed to the American League's integrity and decided that both Cobb and Speaker should retire quietly. At this point, however, Commissioner Landis decided to investigate the case personally and declared that Cobb and Speaker "have not been, nor are they now found guilty of fixing a game. By no decent system of justice could such a finding be made." Continuing the mission that he began in the terrible "Black Sox" days to keep scandal away from the game at all costs, Landis rescued the reputations of the star players. But, in the process, he buried what remained of the credibility of Ban Johnson.

During the early winter of 1927, Johnson's health became a news story. In fact, he had been battling what turned out to be diabetes since his right foot began to bother him in 1919. From then on, states Eugene Murdock, "one could almost diagram his physical and political decline on the same chart." The humiliation he suffered over the Cobb-Speaker affair left the American League without an effective leader. In January 1927, the owners decided to force Johnson to take "a much-needed rest." "The Observer," in *The Sporting News*, saw this decision as "a knifing that will be as historic as that handed Caesar." After the baseball season ended, Johnson, who had been advised to "be entirely free from all responsibilities" by a Chicago doctor, decided to step down officially—and to reject any payment from the moment he ceased to hold his position as American League president. Writes Harold Seymour:

> It was an ignominious and pathetic end for the man who had for so long been the foremost executive in

Organized Baseball. He had stayed too long. Hindsight suggests that he should have left when the American League owners bypassed him and joined with the National League in electing Landis. He could have stepped down then with more grace and dignity.

Similarly, Eugene Murdock saw

two Ban Johnsons. After 1920 the American League president had passed the zenith of his power and had become an embittered, sick old man. As his health failed and as one humiliation was piled on top of another, he lost the clarity of vision and sureness of judgment that marked his imperial years. He tried to avoid feuding with Landis, but the commissioner would not allow many opportunities to embarrass Johnson to pass by.

By early 1931, Johnson's health had deteriorated to the point at which part of his right foot had to be removed. However, infection had spread too fast and too far, and Johnson would not permit any further amputation. On March 28, in a St. Louis hospital, with "Jen" bedridden back in her hometown in Indiana, he died, in Murdock's words, "a lonely exile." In 1937, Ban Johnson was, with manifest justice, elected to baseball's Hall of Fame at the same time as his old antagonist John McGraw. His plaque reads, simply: "Byron Bancroft Johnson, organizer of the American League and its president from its organization in 1900 until his resignation because of ill health in 1927. A great executive." But he deserves more praise than this. "Ban Johnson was a man with a fertile mind and a genius for organization," writes Murdock, who knows him best. "It is no accident that the so-called 'modern era' in baseball (since 1900) coincides precisely with Johnson's arrival on the scene." At the end, reduced to intense bitterness by the way he had been treated for the last decade of his life, Johnson, with a flash of his great and deeply wounded ego, declared: "Baseball can never repay me for what I have done for it." Johnson was wrong; baseball could have. It just didn't.

Harry Pulliam, Johnson's counterpart in the National League at the time of the "Great Baseball War," the peace, and the establishment of the modern major league arrangement, died two decades earlier, also under tragic circumstances—more tragic, in fact. Pulliam never got used to the maneuverings and caprices of the barons of baseball, his bosses. He was, as a result, according to Harold Seymour, "given to brooding over press criticism, said to be inspired by some of the magnates, and was upset by league problems that crowded in on him." Furthermore, considering the status Ban Johnson had in those days, Pulliam experienced added suffering by the galling knowledge that he was always the other, lesser league president.

A cruel truth regarding a man's fate is that it is sometimes abruptly rerouted by an event that subjectively obtrudes heavily at a particular moment even if it shouldn't mean a great deal by any objective measurement. Pulliam's moment of rerouted fate could be traced back to the tenth inning of a game between the Pittsburgh Pirates and Chicago Cubs (the nickname that had by this time replaced Colts) on September 4, 1908, in the last month of a very tight pennant race involving those two teams and the New York Giants. With two out and Pirate runners on first and third in their home half of the inning, "Honus" Wagner singled in what was apparently the winning run. With the runner from third about to touch the plate and end the game, the runner on first, having taken a few *pro forma* steps toward second, simply wheeled around and, in accordance with the accepted practice of the day, headed for the clubhouse. However, technically, this was a dangerous violation of Rule 59, which stated that

> one run shall be scored every time a base runner, after having touched the first three bases, shall legally

touch the home base before three men are put out;
provided, however, if he reaches home on or during a
play in which the third man be forced out or be put
out before reaching first base, a run shall not count.

All a Chicago player had to do to negate the run scored on
Wagner's hit was to get the ball and touch second, recording
a forceout of the runner from first, who could have advanced
to the next base safely had he bothered to try. Johnny Evers,
Chicago's veteran second baseman, was a smart guy. A real
student of the sport, he was always watching; and he saw the
inconsistency with the rules that, he believed, gave his club
hope to reclaim this game. Evers explained his position vig-
orously, as was his habit, to umpire Hank O'Day, but got no
satisfaction. Then Cubs' owner Charles Murphy got into the
act, filing an official protest with the league office; but President Harry Pulliam denied its validity. Nineteen days later,
the Cubs were playing the Giants, and the same thing happened. With two out and the score tied 1–1 in the ninth
inning, New York managed to get runners on first and third.
Shortstop Al Bridwell then laced a single to center, driving in
the apparent winning run. Nineteen-year-old Fred Merkle,
the runner on first, did the usual thing, running for the
clubhouse without having officially arrived safely at second.
Evers watched Rule 59 violated once more at the expense of
his team. However, neither he nor anyone else could get the
game ball to force out Merkle because it had been thrown in
the stands. Nevertheless, Evers appealed to umpire Hank
O'Day again, grabbed one of the spare balls O'Day was
carrying, stepped on second, and demanded that Merkle be
ruled the run-killing out. McGraw later commented that
"frankly, nobody paid much attention to the squabble. . . .
We even joked in the clubhouse about Evers' effort to put
one over, as he had tried in vain to do in Pittsburgh. And that
ended it." But, it hadn't. The next day, a reporter reached
O'Day in his hotel room and got the incredible news that

Merkle was going to be called out. "But," said the reporter, "that left the score tied. Why didn't you order play resumed?" O'Day's reply was that he had called the game on account of darkness.

O'Day was then called to the New York Athletic Club, where Harry Pulliam lived, to discuss the whole irritating situation. Reserving judgment for several days, Pulliam announced that he was affirming O'Day's call. Merkle was out, the game had ended in a tie and it would have to be replayed. The replay, which turned out to be a play-off game for the National League pennant, went to the Cubs, 4–2. Said McGraw, following the game, "My team merely lost something it had honestly won three weeks ago. This cannot be put too strongly." Pulliam felt severely embarrassed about his role in these events. Criticism of his inconsistent judgment regarding Evers' well-taken point applied to the virtually identical Pittsburgh and New York situations must have struck a very exposed nerve of self-doubt and unhappiness with his career. By February 1909, Pulliam had so obviously begun to fall apart that National League owners, gathered for a meeting in New York, gave him a leave of absence "for reasons of illness." Just before he went off, Pulliam asserted that he was sure "there are enough of the opposition to depose me as President, and, as a matter of fact, I would not regret such action on [the owners'] part. The job is a thankless one for the most part, and the friction that one has to contend with is not worth the trouble." For months, he would not be seen by anyone connected with baseball. Then, on the evening of July 28, the switchboard operator at the New York Athletic Club noted a signal coming from Pulliam's room. When Pulliam failed to respond to her call, she sent a club employee to find out what was going on. The employee found Pulliam stretched out on a sofa with a horrid head wound. On the floor, beside him, was a gun and one empty shell. He had shot himself in the right temple, destroying both his eyes. Incredibly, however, he was still

breathing. The Athletic Club doctor, who responded immediately, estimated that he had been struggling in this condition for the past two hours. Pulliam, only forty years old,
survived the rest of the night, but died the next morning. If
any contmporary still wondered to what degree baseball had
become a high-pressured business, with no safe place for a
soul tortured by the incessant grappling for power, promi-
nence, and profits, the scene of Harry Pulliam's awful expiration in the New York Athletic Club had to be very instructive.

All of the key players on the 1904 pennant-winning
Giants returned the following season and not only repeated
as National League champions, but defeated the Philadelphia Athletics in the 1905 World Series, the first played
under the new "Brush Rules," four games to one. Inter-
estingly, each of these five World Series games was a shutout,
the only time this has ever occurred.

Three of these shutouts belonged to Christy Mathewson.
"Big Six" (meaning "old reliable," a reference to the Big Six
Fire Company, reputedly the best of New York's nineteenth
century volunteer fire outfits) would win a total of only five
times in the four World Series in which he played, but he
would go on to record 373 regular-season victories (tied with
Grover Cleveland "Pete" Alexander for the third highest total
ever) in seventeen years, all but one of these triumphs with
the Giants. In addition to pitching, "Matty" became known
as a writer of baseball commentary and instructional and
inspirational books. However, in truth, Mathewson's contribution to these works was not more than the lucrative lending of his celebrated name to ghost writers Richard K. Fox,
publisher of the *Police Gazette,* and Jack Wheeler, a nationally
known syndicated columnist. During World War I, at the age
of thirty-eight, Mathewson, lending credence to his old image as the all-American boy, resigned as manager of the
Cincinnati Reds and accepted a commission in the Chemical
Warfare Division. Unfortunately, during training, he acci-

dentally inhaled enough chemical gas to create a serious weakness in his lungs. For three years, he managed to maintain his health sufficiently to coach for the Giants, but the cough he had been plagued with since his wartime accident would not subside. Diagnosed as having contracted tuberculosis, Mathewson spent his remaining days in and out of the Saranac Lake, New York, sanatorium, finally succumbing to his illness in 1925 at the age of forty-five. For a man who meant so much to the promotion of the game as a personality and performer, Christy Mathewson was fittingly, in 1936, among the first five inducted into the Hall of Fame. On his plaque appears the statement with which the great majority of hitters in his day would concur: "Matty was master of them all."

Nevertheless, in 1904, "Matty's" pitching partner, Joe McGinnity, had a better year. Although he wasn't able to sustain his status as the best pitcher on the Giant staff, McGinnity had a very distinguished career in New York for four more years, especially in 1906 when he won 27 and lost only 12. He probably was the angriest man on the Giant club when Brush and McGraw cancelled the 1904 World Series. McGinnity figured he might make up at least some of the lost money by playing exhibition games in California that fall, but the team management, which virtually owned players through the reserve clause, would not give him permission. By 1908, the thirty-seven-year-old McGinnity's record had slipped to 11–7, and the next year he was in Newark of the Eastern League as pitcher-manager. Incredibly, the "Iron Man" hurled in 116 minor league games through the next two years, logging over 800 innings. And this wasn't the end either. McGinnity kept walking out to the mound for fifteen more seasons in places such as Tacoma, Butte, Vancouver, Danville, and Dubuque. In 1926, he returned to New York City, more specifically Brooklyn, to coach with the Dodgers. This didn't work out, however, and he moved on to one final campaign as the assistant baseball coach at Williams College. In 1929, the "Iron Man" at last proved mortal, dying of cancer in the home of his daughter in Brooklyn. For so much of his career, it appeared that Joe McGinnity was going to be denied the recognition due him as one of baseball's amazing workhorses. But, in 1946, he was properly acknowledged by being inducted into the Hall of Fame, with the "Iron Man" tribute permanently affixed under his name.

Clark Griffith, "the Old Fox," quit the New York Highlanders 56 games into the 1908 season because of interference, as he saw it, from owners Frank Farrell and Bill Devery. Actually, the Highlanders hadn't done all that well under manager Griffith since their riveting 1904 pennant race against the Boston Pilgrims, finishing sixth, second, and fifth the next three years and headed for last during the 1908 campaign. In fact, the Highlanders, soon to drop their original nickname altogether in favor of the increasingly favored "Yankees," did not win their first American League championship until 1921. In the meantime, Griffith had moved on to other baseball employment. The first post-Highlander job he took was as a scout for Cincinnati; and then, in 1909, he moved onto the Reds' bench for his second managerial stint. But this wasn't much more of a ball club than the Highlanders in those years; so Griffith, desperate for talent, decided to break new recruiting ground and sign two Cubans he had heard about, Rafael Almeida and Armando Marsans. Almeida served the Reds for three years as a reserve infielder, and Marsans played a combined eight years in the majors for four different teams as an outfielder. In 1912, at the age of forty-two, Griffith moved back into the American League as manager of the Washington Senators. At the same time, he leaped at the opportunity offered him to buy a piece of the organization, which he could do only by refinancing his Montana ranch. His effect on the game in Washington was felt immediately, as he conceived the idea of having the President of the United States—William Howard Taft, at the time—throw out the first ball to start the season.

To those who knew Clark Griffith in the heyday of his playing career, all this executive business must have seemed ironic. Back then, while pitching for the National League Chicago club, he was one of the strongest forces urging the creation of a potent union to fight the owners. In fact, sportswriter Joe Campbell then called him—with reference to the favorite cause of the radical Populist movement of the 1890s and the leading political and union firebrands of the day— "the free silver politico-pitcher of the Colts, supporter of [William Jennings] Bryan, [Eugene V.] Debs and ["Pitchfork Ben"] Tillman." By 1919, Griffith and Philadelphia grain dealer William Richardson owned 80 percent of the Senators' stock. After the 1920 season, Griffith traded the manager's position for the club presidency. The highest his team had finished was second, three times. Now others would get their chance on the field, although since the Senators remained a second-division team—with the notable exception of the league championship years of 1925 and 1933—Griffith had to bear that painful old saw about Washington being "first in war, first in peace, and last in the American League." Following a sixth-place finish in 1937, the same man who opened the door to Cuban ballplayers took another interesting initiative in looking beyond the usual recruiting areas. In an interview with Sam Lacy of the *Washington Tribune,* a black weekly, the owner-president declared that "there are few big-league magnates who are not aware of the fact that the time is not far off when colored players will take their places beside those of other races in the major leagues." After witnessing twenty-seven-year-old catcher Josh Gibson of the Homestead Grays hit three home runs in one game—including a 460-foot shot into the left field bleachers of Washington's "Griffith

Stadium"—Griffith asked to see him and Walter "Buck" Leonard, the thirty-one-year-old first baseman from the same team. "He asked us," Buck recalled,

> "Do you fellas want to play major-league ball?"
> "Yeah, we wanna play major-league ball."
> "Do you think you could make it?"
> "Yeah, we thinks we could make it."
> "So, well, I tell ya," he says, "if we start takin' colored into the major leagues, we gonna take your best ones and that's gonna break up your league."
> I said, "Well, if that's gonna be better for the players, then it's all right by me."
> But he never did make us an offer, and nothing ever come of it.

Thinking the matter over, Griffith decided not to go through with it. Robert Peterson, in his fascinating work on the Negro leagues, states that "Josh Gibson and Walter F. (Buck) Leonard were the Ruth and Gehrig, the Mantle and Maris of Negro baseball. From 1937 until Gibson's last season in 1946, they were the most feared No. 3 and 4 batting combination in black baseball." That they would have been stars in Washington was a certainty. What a tremendous loss for major league baseball and for the Senators. Recognized for their superior talents, both were, in 1972, inducted together into the Hall of Fame, Gibson posthumously, having died so terribly early of a stroke at the age of thirty-five.

Although Clark Griffith and his wife Ann had no children of their own, they adopted those belonging to Ann's brother. One of them, Calvin, succeeded Clark as president of the Senators when in October 1955, the old man—then in his eighty-sixth year—died of a stomach hemorrhage in Washington. In 1946, "the Old Fox" was voted into the Hall of Fame for his sixty-four years of service to major league baseball as player, manager, president, and owner.

Roy Campanella, the great Brooklyn Dodger catcher of

the 1950s, once noted that "to play this game good, a lot of you has got to be a little boy." No better example can be offered of the "little boy" succeeding in baseball than Willie Keeler. He began life as the son of a horsecar driver and trolley track switchman in Brooklyn; and, despite a notable shift in his career for five years to Baltimore, playing for Hanlon's Orioles, and the opportunities afforded by his celebrity status as one of the game's most complete players, he never moved his residence from the extremely modest family house—some called it a "shack"—on 376 Pulaski Street in his old home borough. In contrast to his daring on the ball field, "Wee Willie" was basically introverted and never married. When Clark Griffith left the Highlanders in 1908, Frank Farrell and Bill Devery had Keeler in mind as his replacement. But, Willie, who knew this, took off so that he wouldn't have to speak to the Highlander owners about a responsible leadership job he didn't believe he could handle. Yet, there were times when Keeler, in a boyish fashion, made a spectacle of himself. For instance, Fred Lieb recalled his special way of celebrating the Fourth of July. Keeler would take his position in right field with a revolver loaded with blanks sticking out of his back pocket. "At regular intervals during the game, Willie would empty his revolver into the sky." He played a total of nineteen years, and, at the end, had an incredible .345 batting average—fifth highest in baseball history. His last year in the majors, 1910, was spent hitting .300 as a pinch hitter for McGraw's Giants. The next year saw him in Toronto of the Eastern League, where he slipped to what was, for him, an embarrassing .277, and so, too far from Brooklyn anyway, he called it quits. For the rest of his active life, he coached and scouted here and there, but, by 1922, was too ill to attend a gigantic parade and banquet given by the city of Baltimore to its old Orioles. Keeler remained confined to his old Brooklyn house for another year, dying in 1923, at the age of fifty. In 1939, he was voted into the Hall of Fame, in which his famous advice, "Hit 'em where they ain't!" appears just below his likeness, followed by the justifiable claim that he was "baseball's greatest place hitter [and] best bunter."

But the finest of them all that 1904 season was the strong man from North Adams, Massachusetts, "Happy Jack" Chesbro. He threw in a league-leading 55 games, starting 51 and completing 48, and totaled 454.2 innings. His 41 wins (against just 12 losses), .774 winning percentage, and 6.69 hits per game also represented the league's best—and no one ever won as many ever again! As the battle for the pennant drew to its excruciatingly tense climax, it was Chesbro who, time after time, was handed the ball. It seems fair to say that the fundamental reason his club was playing for the American League championship on the last day of the season was that he had labored so hard to bring them there. Perhaps his sacrifice—all the effort he put into all those tough pitches in all those critical games—was not worth it in a personal way. He would never have another year nearly that good. In 1905, he slipped to 19–13, but rebounded a little bit the following year with a record of 24–16. By 1909, he had a total of 197 wins in the major leagues and wanted 3 more badly before he was finished. Unfortunately, in nine appearances with the Highlanders that season, he lost three times; and, after New York released him, he appeared once for his home state Boston Red Sox (formerly the Pilgrims), losing that one as well. Recognizing that his baseball career was over, Chesbro went back to northwestern Massachusetts, where he came from, and established a chicken farm. For a time he also coached baseball at nearby Amherst College and pitched a little semi-pro ball. In 1924, he returned to the majors for a few weeks as a coach for Clark Griffith's Washington Senators, but big-league baseball for him could never be more than a frustrating reminder of two negative experiences he could not get over: first, the three games he couldn't win to attain 200 victories; and second, and much more significant, the notorious wild pitch that took on mythic proportions in his mind and the minds of many of his contemporaries.

Since it was a spitball that got away in that horrific ninth inning of the first game of the double-header that cost the Highlanders the 1904 pennant, a movement was begun to get rid of the unsavory thing. In 1909, John B. Foster, editor of the *Spalding Guide*—"Father" Chadwick having died in 1908—organized a "spitball symposium" to make the case against the pitch. Most of the contributors, according to baseball historian and statistician Bill James, "cited the danger of one getting away and someone being hurt as one of the reasons for their opinion." Nevertheless, it was not until 1920 that the spitball was banned, except for use by eighteen pitchers who had relied upon it heavily. When Burleigh Grimes retired in 1934, the spitball was never supposed to be thrown again.

Meanwhile, back in Conway, Massachusetts, Chesbro was, until his death in November 1931, forever asked about "the wild pitch." It became the stuff of nightmares for him. That one baseball that slipped from his grip effectively ruined the rest of his life. However, as ghastly a thing as it was for him, it represented just one of thousands of interesting reminders of the long and colorful history of baseball that were accepted for display by Cooperstown's Hall of Fame. Chesbro, himself, was admitted to the gallery of the game's greatest performers in 1946, his plaque placed among those of the other notables on the first floor. But one short flight up the stairs, in a case full of mementos of happy occasions for players of Chesbro's era, in the front along the right-hand side, lies the bane of the last twenty-seven years of his existence. It doesn't seem probable that this little round object could have caused such damage. But then the place in American popular culture achieved by the game Alexander Joy Cartwright refined into baseball isn't probable either. And the place of its annual World Series is even less probable—annual, that is, except for 1904, when John Brush and John McGraw called it off.

Bibliography

BASEBALL RECORD BOOKS

Carter, Craig, ed. *The Complete Baseball Record Book.* St. Louis: The Sporting News Publishing Co., 1986.

Chadwick, Henry, ed. *Spalding's Official Base Ball Guide, 1903.* New York: American Sports Publishing Co., 1903.

———. *Spalding's Official Base Ball Guide, 1904.* New York: American Sports Publishing Co., 1904.

———. *Spalding's Official Base Ball Guide, 1905.* New York: American Sports Publishing Co., 1905.

Nemec, David, ed. *Great Baseball Feats, Facts and Firsts.* New York: New American Library, 1987.

Reichler, Joseph L., ed. *Fabulous Baseball Facts, Feats and Firsts.* New York: Collier Books, 1981.

———. *The Baseball Encyclopedia.* New York: Macmillan Publishing Co., 1982.

———. *The Great All-Time Baseball Record Book.* New York: Macmillan Publishing Co., 1981.

Richter, Francis C., ed. *Reach's Official American League Base Ball Guide for 1903.* Philadelphia: A.J. Reach Co., 1903.

———. *Reach's Official American League Base Ball Guide for 1904.* Philadelphia: A.J. Reach Co., 1904.

————. *Reach's Official American League Base Ball Guide for 1905.* Philadelphia: A.J. Reach Co., 1905.

OTHER WORKS

Alexander, Charles C. *Ty Cobb.* New York: Oxford University Press, 1984.

Allen, Lee. *The American League Story.* New York: Hill & Wang, 1962.

————. *The National League Story.* New York: Hill & Wang, 1961.

Anderson, Dave. *The Yankees.* New York: Random House, 1980.

Appel, Martin, and Burt Goldblatt. *Baseball's Best: The Hall of Fame Gallery.* New York: McGraw-Hill Publishing Co., 1980.

Berry, Henry. *Baseball's Great Teams: Boston Red Sox.* New York: Rutledge Books, 1975.

Bowman, John S., and Joel Zoss. *The American League.* London: Bison Books, 1986.

————. *The National League.* London: Bison Books, 1986.

Brasher, William. *Josh Gibson, A Life in the Negro Leagues.* New York: Harper & Row, Publishers, 1978.

Cobb, Ty, and Al Stump. *My Life in Baseball, The True Record.* Garden City, NY: Doubleday, 1961.

Collett, Ritter. *The Cincinnati Reds, A Pictorial History of Professional Baseball's Oldest Team.* Norfolk, VA: Teagle & Little, 1976.

Connable, Aldred, and Edward Silberfarb. *Tigers of Tammany, Nine Men Who Ran New York.* New York: Holt, Rinehart and Winston, 1967.

Creamer, Robert W. *Babe, The Legend Comes to Life.* New York: Penguin Books, 1983.

————. *Stengel, His Life and Times.* New York: Simon & Schuster, 1984.

Cudahy, Brian J. *Under the Sidewalks of New York.* Battleboro, VT: The Stephen Greene Press, 1979.

Curran, William. *Mitts, A Celebration of the Art of Fielding.* New York: William Morrow & Company, 1985.

Danzig, Allison, and Joseph L. Reichler. *The History of Baseball, Its Great Players, Teams, and Managers.* Englewood Cliffs, NJ: Prentice-Hall, 1959.

Davids, L. Robert, ed. *Insider's Baseball.* New York: Charles Scribner's Sons, 1983.

Dickey, Glenn. *The History of American League Baseball Since 1901.* New York: Stein & Day, 1980.

————. *The History of National League Baseball Since 1876.* New York: Stein & Day, 1979.

————. *The History of the World Series Since 1903.* New York: Stein & Day, 1984.

Durant, John. *Highlights of the World Series.* New York: Hastings House, 1971.

Durso, Joseph. *The Days of Mr. McGraw.* Englewood Cliffs, NJ: Prentice-Hall, 1969.

Einstein, Charles, ed. *The Baseball Reader.* New York: McGraw-Hill Publishing Company, 1980.

————. *The Fireside Book of Baseball.* New York: Simon & Schuster, 1956.

————. *The Second Fireside Book of Baseball.* New York: Simon & Schuster, 1958.

————. *The Third Fireside Book of Baseball.* New York: Simon & Schuster, 1968.

Ellis, Edward Robb. *The Epic of New York City.* New York: Coward-McCann, 1966.

Evers, John J., and Hugh S. Fullerton. *Touching Second, The Science of Baseball.* Chicago: The Reilly & Britton Company, 1910.

Falls, Joe. *Baseball's Great Teams: Detroit Tigers.* New York: Rutledge Books, 1975.

Goldstone, Harmon H., and Martha Dalrymple. *History Preserved, A Guide to New York City Landmarks and Historic Districts.* New York: Schocken Books, 1976.

Graham, Frank. *The Brooklyn Dodgers, An Informal History.* New York: G.P. Putnam's Sons, 1945.

————. *McGraw of the Giants.* New York: G.P. Putnam's Sons, 1944.

Holmes, Tommy. *Baseball's Great Teams: The Dodgers.* New York: Rutledge Books, 1975.

Honig, Donald. *The American League, An Illustrated History.* New York: Crown Publishers, 1983.

————. *The Boston Red Sox, An Illustrated Tribute.* New York: St. Martin's Press, 1984

————. *The National League, An Illustrated History.* New York: Crown Publishers, 1983.

Hynd, Noel. *The Giants of the Polo Grounds.* New York: Doubleday, 1988.

James, Bill. *The Bill James Historical Baseball Abstract*. New York: Villard Books, 1986.

Kaese, Harold. *The Boston Braves*. New York: G.P. Putnam's Sons, 1948.

Kahn, James M. *The Umpire Story*. New York: G.P. Putnam's Sons, 1953.

Klein, Aaron E. *The History of the New York Central System*. New York: Bonanza Books, 1985.

Kouwenhoven, John A. *The Columbia Historical Portrait of New York*. New York: Harper & Row, Publishers, 1972.

Leitner, Irving A. *Baseball: Diamond in the Rough*. New York: Criterion Books, 1972.

Lewis, Franklin. *The Cleveland Indians*. New York: G.P. Putnam's Sons, 1949.

Lieb, Frederick G. *Baseball As I Have Known It*. New York: Coward, McCann & Geohegan, 1977.

———. *The Baltimore Orioles*. New York: G.P. Putnam's Sons, 1955.

———. *The Baseball Story*. New York: G.P. Putnam's Sons, 1950.

———. *The Pittsburgh Pirates*. New York: G.P. Putnam's Sons, 1948.

———. *The Story of the World Series*. New York: G.P. Putnam's Sons, 1965.

Lowenfish, Lee, and Tony Lupien. *The Imperfect Diamond: The Story of Baseball's Reserve System and the Men Who Fought To Change It*. New York: Stein & Day, 1980.

Lowry, Philip J. *Green Cathedrals*. Cooperstown, NY: Society for American Baseball Research, 1986.

Lyman, Susan Elizabeth. *The Story of New York, An Informal History of the City*. New York: Corwin Publishers, 1964.

Mackay, Donald A. *The Building of Manhattan*. New York: Harper & Row, Publishers, 1987.

Marazzi, Richard. *The Rules and Lore of Baseball*. New York: Stein & Day, 1980.

McGraw, Blanche, and Arthur Mann. *The Real McGraw*. New York: David McKay Co., 1953.

McGraw, John J. *My Thirty Years in Baseball*. New York: Boni and Liveright, 1923.

Miller, Rita Seiden, ed. *Brooklyn U.S.A.*. Brooklyn, NY: Brooklyn College Press, 1979.

Morris, Lloyd. *Incredible New York, High Life and Low Life of the Last Hundred Years*. New York: Random House, 1951.

Murdock, Eugene C. *Ban Johnson, Czar of Baseball.* Westport, CT: Greenwood Press, 1982.

Nash, Bruce, and Allan Zullo. *The Baseball Hall of Shame.* New York: Pocket Books, 1985.

Okrent, Daniel, and Harris Lewine, ed. *The Ultimate Baseball Book.* Boston: The Hilltown Press, 1981.

Peterson, Harold. *The Man Who Invented Baseball.* New York: Charles Scribner's Sons, 1973.

Peterson, Robert. *Only the Ball Was White.* New York: McGraw-Hill Publishing Company, 1984.

Peterson, Virgil W. *The Mob, 200 Years of Organized Crime in New York.* Ottawa, IL: Green Hill Publishers, 1983.

Quigley, Martin. *The Crooked Pitch: The Curveball in American Baseball.* Chapel Hill, NC: Algonquin Books, 1984.

Reichler, Joseph L. *The Baseball Trade Register.* New York: Collier Books, 1984.

———. *The Game and the Glory.* Englewood Cliffs, NJ: Prentice-Hall, 1976.

———. *The World Series.* New York: Simon & Schuster, 1978.

Reidenbaugh, Lowell. *Baseball's Hall of Fame, Cooperstown, Where the Legends Live Forever.* New York: Arlington House, 1983.

———. *100 Years of National League Baseball, 1876–1976.* St. Louis: The Sporting News Publishing Co., 1976.

Reynolds, Donald M. *The Architecture of New York City.* New York: Macmillan Publishing Co., 1984.

Riess, Steven. *Touching Base: Professional Baseball and American Culture in the Progressive Era.* Westport, CT: Greenwood Press, 1980.

Ritter, Lawrence S. *The Glory of Their Times: The Story of the Early Days of Baseball Told by the Men Who Played It.* New York: Macmillan Publishing Co., 1966.

Schlossberg, Dan. *The Baseball Catalog.* Middle Village, NY: Jonathan David Publishers, 1983.

Seymour, Harold. *Baseball, the Early Years.* New York: Oxford University Press, 1960.

———. *Baseball, the Golden Age.* New York: Oxford University Press, 1971.

Shannon, Bill, and George Kalinsky. *The Ballparks.* New York: Hawthorn Books, 1975.

Smith, Robert. *Baseball.* New York: Simon & Schuster, 1970.

———. *Baseball in America.* New York: Holt, Rinehart and Winston, 1961.

Suehsdorf, A. D. *The Great American Baseball Scrapbook.* New York: Rutledge Books, 1978.

Sullivan, George. *The Picture History of the Boston Red Sox.* New York: The Bobbs-Merrill Company, 1979.

——— and John Powers. *Yankees, An Illustrated History.* Englewood Cliffs, NJ: Prentice-Hall, 1982.

Tauranac, John. *Essential New York.* New York: Holt, Rinehart and Winston, 1979.

Thorn, John, and Pete Palmer. *The Hidden Game of Baseball.* Garden City, NY: Doubleday, 1985.

———. *The National Pastime.* New York: Warner Books, 1987.

Voigt, David Quentin. *American Baseball: From Gentleman's Sport to the Commissioner System.* Norman, OK: University of Oklahoma Press, 1966.

———. *American Baseball: From the Commissioners to Continental Expansion.* University Park, PA: Pennsylvania State University, 1983.

Wallop, Douglass. *Baseball, An Informal History.* New York: Bantam Books, 1969.

Wolfe, Gerard R. *New York, A Guide to the Metropolis.* New York: McGraw-Hill Publishing Co., 1988.

W.P.A. Guide to New York City. New York: Pantheon Books, 1982.

JOURNALS AND PERIODICALS

Baseball History

Boston Herald

Brooklyn Daily Eagle

Chicago Daily Tribune

Indianapolis Star Magazine

New York Daily Tribune

New York Herald

New York World

Sporting Life

The Baseball Magazine

The Baseball Research Journal

The National Pastime

The New York Times

The Sporting News

Index

NEW YORK
NATIONAL
Champion
1904